BARBARA MILO OHRBACH

Tabletops

EASY, PRACTICAL, BEAUTIFUL
WAYS TO DECORATE THE TABLE

PHOTOGRAPHS BY JOHN HALL

CLARKSON POTTER/PUBLISHERS
NEW YORK

Copyright © 1997 by
Barbara Milo Ohrbach

Published by
Clarkson N. Potter, Inc.
201 East 50th Street,
New York, New York 10022.
Member of the Crown
Publishing Group.

Printed in China

Design by Dania Martinez Davey

Calligraphy by Joann Owen Coy

Random House, Inc.
New York, Toronto, London,
Sydney, Auckland

http//www.randomhouse.com/

Clarkson N. Potter,
Potter, and colophon
are trademarks of
Clarkson N. Potter, Inc.

Library of Congress
Cataloging
in-Publication
Data is available
upon request

ISBN 0-517-70332-7

10 9 8 7 6 5 4 3 2 1

First Edition

Publisher's Note: This book contains several recipes using botanicals. Some of these may cause allergic
reactions in some individuals, so reasonable care in preparation is advised.

*"You must come home with me and be my guest; You will give joy to me,
and I will do all that is in my power to honour you."*

—Percy Bysshe Shelley

ACKNOWLEDGMENTS

It is always a pleasure and honor to work with exceptionally talented people—especially if they are as enthusiastic, committed, and generous as these—John Hall, my photographer; Dania Martinez Davey, my designer; and Deborah Geltman and Gayle Benderoff—thank you for making this book a reality.

During the several years it took to put *Tabletops* together, the wonderful people listed here shared their beautiful homes, creative ideas, and gracious hospitality with me:

John and Beth Allen, Ted and Lillie Anastasakis, Michael Anderson, Garance Aufaure, Sig Bergamin, Roberta Bernstein, Bruce and Bonnie Caputo, Karen Carroll, Rita Cerchia, Joe Cicio, Jean Clayton, Sara Coleman, Dr. and Mrs. Henry Crommelin, Jr., Sue Cutler, Lynn Dodson, Sandy Ericson, Mary Catherine Faircloth, Mike Feldman and Adrienne Arsht, Randi Foreman, The Honorable and Ms. Joseph Gildenhorn, Doris Goddard, Godiva Chocolates, Gump's, Maeva Gyenes, David Hezlep, Jane Hawkins Hoke, Cathy Horton, Dorothy Ireland, Stephen and Joanne Isola, Sheryl Isobe and Carolyn Drennen, Linda Johnson and Ann Hull, Marjorie H. Johnston, Harold and Nancy Klein, Al and Vie Koerner, Cynthia Lanpher, Robert and Joy Lewis, Jean and Marty Markovitz, Sarah Mauro, Patricia McCarthy, Kathy G. Mezrano of Kathy G's & Co., Caterers, Malcolm Mokotoff, Kevin Monogue, Benjamin Noriega-Ortiz, Tom Mathieu, Cathleen McFarland, Sara McGregor, Eric Michael, William Mihans, Julie Nass, Offray Ribbons, Russ O'Quinn,

Vasos and Kathy Papagapitos, Katherine Pearson, Jane Perin, Penne Poole Interiors, Diana Quasha, Jorge and Annette Rodriguez, Mark Rose, Nancy Rosenbloom, Claudia Aronow-Roush, Marjory Salick, Antonia Bakker Salvato, Samson Fine Arts, Ellie Schneider, Claudia Seipp and Deborah Barbour, Doreen Sepe, Gail Serfaty, The White House Reception Rooms, Sandra Schneider, Julie Schroeder, Stephanie Schus, Marjory Segal, Margy Shultz, Ann Standrod, Arnold and Rose Steiner, Jim and Mary Margaret Todd, Barrie Vanderpoel, Lisa Van Der Reijden, Elsie Wagner, J. Watkins, Nan Whalen, Williams-Sonoma, The Women's Committee for the National Symphony Orchestra, Washington, D.C., and Ann Yanaway.

Special gratitude to Patricia Sadowsky, a friend indeed, who always knew what I was looking for—and found it. Thanks to Robert and Kay Lautman and John and Marilyn Hannigan for the "Cherishable" photographs.

Deep appreciation to my editor, Annetta Hanna, and all the people at Clarkson Potter for all their hard work and dedication: Amy Boorstein, Mary Ellen Briggs, Paula Cohen, Joan Denman, Jo Fagan, Chip Gibson, Robbin Gourley, Debbie Koenig, Ed Otto, Elaine Panagides, Andrea Peabbles, Christian Red, Wendy Schuman, Lauren Shakely, Gayle Shanks, Laurie Stark, Robin Strashun, Rebecca Strong, Jane Treuhaft, and Sean Yule.

I don't remember who said that it's the journey, not the arrival that matters, but in this case it was true. It is with much love that I acknowledge the assistance and support of my husband, Mel, who always makes a difficult journey possible—and fun.

AMITIE

CONTENTS

Introduction

welcome · hospitality · beauty

"The way in which meal times are passed," wrote the French gastronome Anthelme Brillat-Savarin, "is most important to what happiness we find in life." When I was growing up in the 1950s, it seemed that we were always sitting at the table. My father got home from work at 6:00 P.M., and we had dinner at 6:30. As a result, my sister and I missed the end of every movie on "The Early Show."

Every Sunday, we had dinner with one or the other set of grandparents. These midday meals, with various aunts, uncles, and cousins, afforded more drama, histrionics, and humor than any movie we could have seen!

≥ OPPOSITE: The front entrance to our stone carriage house. At right is the porch, which faces green mountains in the distance. It's a lovely, cool spot to welcome guests and to sit on summer evenings, watching the fireflies and enjoying relaxed dinners and good conversation.
ABOVE: This charming needlepoint doorstop from my collection says it all!
FOLLOWING PAGES: Our country kitchen has seen many happy family meals. My Staffordshire plates adorn walls as well as the table. The pineapple says "welcome," and the pitchers filled with wheat symbolize the bounty of the garden.

They were all-day affairs. I remember long tables, lots of commotion, chattering adults and noisy children, mountains of delicious food, much laughter and sometimes tears.

As children, we always looked forward to these Sundays surrounded by loving relatives who "let us get away with murder," as my mother put it. They pinched our cheeks, told us how adorable we were, and slipped us a sip of red wine when no one was looking, along with a shiny quarter as we were leaving. Unfortunately, like so many other wonderful family rituals, the tradition of Sunday dinner gradually became only a dim memory.

Years later, when I was married, my husband and I fell in love with an old carriage house in the country. It was an impulsive purchase. All those empty rooms, all that land—what would we do with it? We soon got our answer. Six nieces and nephews, including twins age two, arrived from the Far East to spend the summer with us and continued to do so for the next fifteen years.

My parents joined us too, and for more than three months every year, we never cooked a meal for less than ten people! I often think of those summers and of

1

🦋 ABOVE LEFT: When guests are invited, the thing I love best is decorating the table. Here I am, just starting out with a woven cutlery basket I found in one of London's wonderful antiques markets.

ABOVE RIGHT: This is a favorite table setting of mine using a mixture of the early Canton, Mason, and Staffordshire china I have collected over the years. Mother-of-pearl and silver flatware, crisp antique damask, and lush peonies and roses from the garden complete the picture.

what Laurie Colwin wrote in her book *More Home Cooking:* "The table is a meeting place, a gathering ground, the source of sustenance and nourishment, festivity, safety, and satisfaction."

Ours was all those things, and more. There was always a properly set table (we had lots of little hands) and flowers from the garden or field. And there was usually entertainment, skits made up on the spur of the moment or games like Monopoly, where we had to keep a sharp eye on the miniature bankers!

But even though the children are now grown—in college and working—we continue to entertain them and a constantly changing group of friends and relatives. The center of our home life still revolves around the same country table that has seen so many happy meals. And in addition to good food and good fellowship, I still want our table to look as beautiful as it possibly can.

One way I've tried to achieve this is with flowers. How the table is decorated sends an unspoken message of hospitality—a sentiment conveyed by the flowers even when the meal is a simple one served on everyday dishes.

"Hospitality," the dictionary says, "is the entertainment of guests with generous kindness." Despite the fact that we have less time, everyone seems to be entertaining more at home. There never seems to be enough time to do everything properly. Yet there *are* many solutions that don't take extraordinary talent or creativity to achieve. In fact, the most simple is usually the most elegant.

After I wrote *Simply Flowers,* I received countless letters asking for more ideas for decorating the table. So I decided to do *Tabletops.* It is filled with what I hope are practical, easy, yet clever suggestions for making tables look pretty. These include using everything from wildflowers and vegetables to your children's artwork on tables for breakfast, lunch, or dinner.

Since the table is a place where joyous times are shared by all, this should be reflected in the way we approach decorating it. My philosophy is have a good time. Do things naturally. Stop worrying. Decorating the table should be a creative endeavor that gives us satisfaction.

The first chapter, "Starting Out," discusses coordinating tableware so that everything works together with the centerpiece. Accessories like candles, napkin rings, and place cards are featured in Chapter 2, "Beautiful Details."

"Choosing Containers" and "Creating Centerpieces" are the main focus of the book. Making leaf vases and centerpieces, and preparing your botanicals are all included here. "Setting Tables Inside" and "Setting Tables Outside," are the two chapters that put everything into context within rooms and out in the open air. "Using Flowers in Food" covers imaginative ways to use edible flowers.

I always enjoy decorating our house at festive times of the year, so the next chapters, "Celebrating Christmas" and "Special Occasions," are filled with fun ideas and how-to recipes, many that you can do with children, for Christmas, holidays, and special occasions.

"Finding Inspiration," the last chapter, discusses where I get ideas for *my* tabletops: Historic homes, restaurants, and farmers' markets are all grist for the mill if you know what to look for. In the "Source Guide," I follow up by sharing my special lists of favorite spots, including tabletop shops carrying new and antique tableware; florist and floral supply sources; and homes and gardens to visit.

A last thought before you turn the page: By creating nurturing surroundings, especially at the table, you are really brightening your little corner of the world. The pleasures of the table, whether they consist of a simple meal or a feast, decorated with daisies or rare orchids, should be a blending of satisfying food, friendship, graciousness, and warmth, all sparked with the glow of fine conversation and lots of laughter. I once read that hospitality is not a contest; it is *sharing* the best that you have with those you love and enjoy being with—and I agree.

Bon appétit!
Barbara Milo Ohrbach

RIGHT: Whenever I start working on a book, I organize the artwork that I have gathered in my research. It inspires me. Some of these engravings are quite old—the colored ones are from an antique cookbook that's over 150 years old. The Victorian gallery glass, which was used to look closely at pictures hung in exhibitions, makes a handy magnifier.

Chapter 1

🦋 LEFT: Several days
before guests are
expected, I like to plan
what I will use on the
table. Being considered
in this case are some old
silver pieces, etched
glass plates, stemware,
and crisp damask
napkins. Then I
coordinate the flowers,
perhaps peonies.
FOLLOWING PAGE: I have
many antique serving
pieces, but I don't have
self-control or storage
space! So I use every
place available,
including an eighteenth-
century French
cupboard that doubles
as a buffet and
hydrangea drying shelf.
DETAIL: A favorite
diamond-shaped serving
dish from England, circa
1860, with hand-colored
fruits in the center.

Starting Out

linen • silver • glass • china

"We took great pride in preparing and serving meals for company, and while we didn't have the best china, you'd be surprised what you can do with fresh flowers and pressed linens." I so enjoyed reading *Having Our Say,* by sisters Sara and Elizabeth Delany, and appreciated their philosophy about table setting and entertaining—and life!

How many ways are there to set a table? Many. To be beautiful, all depend upon a tasteful combination of china, glassware, silver, table linens, and, most important, the centerpieces. With this abundance of choices, it is important to plan ahead when you begin to think about decorating the table—it shouldn't be a last-minute thing.

I always begin by reviewing what I already have. I have loved and collected blue and white dishes from the time I was first married; when I buy something new, it must coordinate with my existing china. This way, however creative I feel, I know it will all work together. A few points to always remember: Color unifies everything. Keep things manageable. It's important that you be able to cope with the planning and enjoy the meal. Setting the table should be a pleasure and fun if

you approach it sensibly. Here are some more specific suggestions:

The **tablecloth** you choose will determine the overall mood of your finished table setting and establish the degree of formality. The cloth should generously overhang the table. I like using two, a drop cloth to the floor with the tablecloth, chosen for the meal, over it. I prefer solid-colored cloths, like white damask, batiste, or linen, because most of my china is patterned.

Place mats and **runners** allow for versatility, as they come in different sizes and many materials, and can be used atop a bare table. Mats are used for less formal meals and I find they also come in handy when protecting delicate textiles like the old quilts and paisley shawls that I like to use. Remember that the *entire* place setting should fit on the mat, and that the mats should not overlap.

I probably have more **napkins** than anything else. They come in lots of patterns and colors, and can easily change the look of the table. Sometimes I even buy brightly colored dish towels to use as napkins for picnics and other casual meals. Napkins come in many sizes, such as six inches for cocktail, sixteen inches

One white plate—3 ways

For me, a white plate is like an empty canvas—the possibilities are endless! With this versatile classic, you can create a variety of moods just by changing the linens and accessories. Then coordinating the centerpiece is simple. Choose a design that will go with what you own from the big selection available in many stores in white or cream shades.

1. An all-white table setting is always clean and sparkling fresh. It looks good when done with casual tableware as well as with the more traditional pieces shown here. By using all white flowers—lisianthus and button mums—in a clear vase, the green of the stems and leaves becomes a fresh accent.

2. How different everything looks just by adding color. I often use woven jacquard mats and napkins in addition to a simple cloth. The blue glass goblets provide a focal point. I like arranging blue flowers with deep orange ones, here, delphiniums, daylilies, and roses in an antique pitcher.

3. You'll hardly recognize the white plate now, surrounded as it is by bright, vivid colors. Inexpensive napkins and a multicolored centerpiece of country flowers like daisies, tulips, irises, and daffodils provide a sunny backdrop for a friendly lunch. The fruit salt and pepper shakers are Italian pottery, as is the painted oval cachepot.

for luncheon, and twenty to twenty-four inches for dinner. I prefer oversized ones and I have some favorite Victorian napkins that are twenty-eight inches. Seek out lovely linens at tag sales and antiques shows—and come home with a bargain.

When it comes to **china,** don't be afraid to be original. Today, there is no right or wrong way to use it. It's not necessary that everything match—you can certainly use various patterned dishes as long as they coordinate and are appropriate.

If you are just starting out, get the basics first. And try to buy at least a dozen of each, as china—and even pottery—is fragile. If you choose a pattern that is open stock, you can add one piece at a time and

ABOVE: Besides a water goblet, far right, a separate glass is necessary for each wine: champagne, top left, red and white, all in Waterford crystal.

BELOW: Follow certain rules for setting the table: forks on the left, spoons and knives (with blades inward) to the right. Bring dessert spoons and forks to the table with dessert or place them above the plate when setting the table. Utensils are always placed in the order they will be used, working from the outside to the center. In this case, salad will be served first. Place the dinner plate one inch from the table's edge; bread-and-butter plate above forks; water goblet directly above knife tip; wineglasses to the right.

🦋 Though the five-piece place setting (asterisked here) includes the basics, I like having some additional pieces. All are shown in Tiffany's Hampton pattern. LEFT TO RIGHT: dessert fork, salad fork,* dinner fork,* dinner knife,* dessertspoon, bouillon or soup spoon,* teaspoon,* and demitasse spoon.

other sizes later. The pieces most frequently used are the dinner plate, salad plate, soup bowl, cup and saucer, and bread-and-butter plate. Colored or clear-glass plates have many uses. I find they come in handy when I have a large group of people to feed. I also like to collect serving pieces in unusual shapes to dress up the table.

There are three types of **flatware:** sterling silver, silver plate, and stainless steel. Some people have two sets, one in sterling, for special occasions, and one of the latter for everyday use.

The choice of contemporary silver patterns can be bewildering. Many of us are lucky enough to have inherited family silver. And for those who haven't, there is an abundance of old flatware available from the Victorian era, since a meal then could have ten courses. This makes collecting silver a real opportunity. For interest and utility, add fish knives and forks, butter spreaders, and other pieces to your table setting. And since silver companies at the turn of the century manufactured over 150 different types of serving pieces, you will have no trouble finding things like salad servers, cake knives, and soup ladles. They don't need to match! The photograph on this page illustrates the basic silver you need to start out with.

Glass lends grace and elegance to the table. The choice of stemware sizes, shapes, and colors is endless, and each serves a distinct purpose. It is important to have the fundamentals, however, before branching out to the other options.

Crystal, handblown, and pressed glass are your three choices. Glasses break more frequently than anything else, so start with a least a dozen of each size. The shapes you will need depend on your taste and style of entertaining—at minimum two glasses, one for water and a multipurpose wineglass. If you serve both red and white wines, you will need one glass for red and a smaller one for white. Champagne flutes are also important.

If you lay out your china, flatware,

and glasses in advance, like a dress rehearsal, you will eliminate anxiety. You can then appreciate unfolding freshly laundered cloths and creamy napkins as you start to prepare for your guests.

Your tableware should be looked after properly and my book *Antiques at Home* has a section in each chapter with suggestions on caring for it. Here are some basic tips:

Table Linens
• Hand wash in warm water with a neutral detergent. Rinse well in clear water.
• Don't use chlorine bleach.
• Store table linens flat, never on hangers and never in plastic bags. Fold in acid-free tissue to prevent yellowing.

Glass and China
• Dust with a soft, thick watercolor brush.
• Never put antiques in a dishwasher.
• Before washing, line the sink with a rubber pad or towels.
• Don't crowd too many objects on a shelf. Store big objects in back, small ones in front.

Silver and Serving Pieces
• When polishing, use a sponge and nonabrasive foam cleaner.
• If the piece is slightly tarnished, wash it in soapy water instead of polishing. Dry at once.
• Store silver in airtight plastic or special silver bags to retard tarnishing.

OPPOSITE: In summer, I enjoy hanging my freshly washed table linens outside to dry in the sun. Tablecloths are spread on the dewy lawn. Fragile pieces are dried flat on white towels.

TOP RIGHT: Fine crystal feels balanced when you pick it up. The stem allows you to hold the glass without your hand warming the liquid inside.

CENTER: Use interesting antique serving pieces like these oak-leaf-and-acorn platters and vegetable dishes in Wedgwood's Queens Ware.

BOTTOM: More people are drinking espresso, so demitasse cups and spoons are useful.

🦋 LEFT: I'd be lost
without my box of pretty
ribbons! The sheer
organza ones on this
candelabra change with
the seasons. In winter,
I use green ribbons with
ivy. In summer, the look
is totally different with
pink roses and ribbons.
FOLLOWING PAGE: I always
know what to buy for a
dear friend's birthday—
she collects silver Victorian
napkin rings. They were
made in a great variety
of shapes and were
embossed with designs,
as well as with names,
initials, and dates.
DETAIL: A Victorian brass
place card holder in
the shape of a hand
holds an ornately
embossed name card.

Beautiful Details

ribbons • napkin rings • candles

After reading the wonderful book *A Romantic Education* I discovered what I've been afflicted with all these years!

In it, author Patricia Hampl writes, "'You've got the beauty disease,' a friend of mine said a few years ago, exasperated with me—the flowers, the attention to detail, the domestic fussing with myself and the materials at hand . . . wanting beauty around me."

I think that if you have to have a disease, this is the one to have. You won't need pills or ointments. And aside from little sighs of exasperation from friends and husbands, the only side effect is beauty—not a bad thing in a world that is quickly becoming less and less attractive.

Victor Hugo said, "The beautiful is as useful as the useful, perhaps more so." All of us feel a lot better when surrounded by beauty. It's a necessity. Whether it's natural—woods, flowers, water—or purchased from your favorite emporium, beauty keeps us going.

We could have predicted what the latest studies have shown: Sick people heal much faster when the walls of their hospital rooms are painted in happy, bright colors instead of a drab green, or when the view from their window includes a verdant tree. Beauty heals too!

Focus on beauty when setting the table. The little details make such a difference. Now that you have decided what tableware to use, you can get creative, exploring choices in napkin rings, place cards, candles, candle shades, and fingerbowls. Keeping it simple or not is up to you.

Many years ago, it was considered an honor for a guest to be asked to roll his or her napkin into a napkin ring, as the family did after each meal. This meant it would be set aside for the guest's eagerly awaited next visit. (At that time, it was considered bad manners to really use one's napkin.) Nowadays, **napkin rings** are purely decorative.

You can purchase them made from almost any material. I like old silver ones with dates, people's initials, and figures on them. My Aunt Jeanette, who had a green thumb, was also a very arts and crafts–type person. She made napkin rings from felt, which is a cute, inexpensive idea when you're having lots of people for a holiday buffet or a big birthday party. I also enjoy wrapping napkins with fresh and artificial flowers, fruits, spices, dried leaves, ribbons, trimmings, lace, and raffia.

19

ABOVE: This is part of a collection of charming figural napkin rings that belongs to another friend. Made of silver plate, they were popular during the nineteenth century. Each family member had his or her own, which usually reflected their interests. Other common themes were nursery rhymes and love.

BELOW: Decorating napkins is an easy, fun way to dress up the table. Left to right: A silk rose tucked into a piece of woven ribbon; a fresh daffodil tied with lace; cinnamon sticks and eucalyptus leaves wrapped with raffia; a bunch of violets with a narrow picot ribbon; artificial cherries accented with gingham checks.

No-Sew Napkin Ring

4 pieces of 9 x 12-inch felt
Scissors
Cardboard for pattern pieces

1. Make 3 cardboard pattern pieces: napkin loop (1); leaf (2); flower (3).

2. Lay the pattern pieces on the felt as above and cut out:
- napkin loops (1) from each of two pieces of felt—you can use just one color, if desired
- leaf (2) is cut out of green
- flower (3) is cut out of pink

3. Cut a 1-inch cross in the center of the leaf pattern (2), and the flower pattern (3).

4. To assemble: Lay (1) flat and pull the two ends together through the slit of the leaf (2), then through the flower (3). The two hanging ends will be looped around the rolled napkin and pulled through the slit of the leaf and flower, encircling the center of the napkin.

ABOVE: No-Sew Napkin Rings. The dumbbell-shaped piece on the bottom becomes the napkin loop and center of the flower. The green is the leaf pattern and the bright pink is the flower pattern.

Then there is napkin folding. There are many books on the subject, usually with diagrams, so I won't go on about it here, except to say that in seventeenth-century Versailles, where folding techniques reached their apex, napkins were shaped into everything from pyramids to peacocks. If you are so inclined, and creative, the sky is the limit.

Place cards tell us where to sit. At any gathering, the host or hostess should have the seating planned in advance so guests avoid awkward moments and find their places easily—hopefully, sitting next to someone who is a wonderful conversationalist with lots in common with them! Place cards are especially useful at holiday time, so Aunt Dot and Aunt Mary, who aren't speaking again this year, don't end up sitting next to each other.

To help you decide where to put people, seating charts are available. These come with little name cards that can be moved about at will. You can also create a simple diagram on a piece of paper, which is what I usually do.

Place cards come in a range of styles, or you can make your own. For me, it's as much fun to use embossed place cards with calligraphy, as it is to write with a gold felt-tipped pen on leaves or flat stones collected in our field.

The fact that they are quite unnecessary makes the presence of **candles** something special. There is nothing like a room or table glowing with shimmering candlelight to set a festive or romantic mood. If you have a chandelier, put it on dimmers so the light is flattering.

Indispensable to a gracious table, candles used in abundance look distinctive when clustered in or among flowers, and groupings of candlesticks in silver, bronze, brass, wood, or glass make a glittering centerpiece on their own. Don't be afraid to use various shapes and sizes together. And don't underestimate the effectiveness of smaller candles at each place setting. They give an intimate feeling to the table.

The candles I use most are small votives in colored glass or silver holders, twelve- to eighteen-inch tapers in off-white or cream, and pillar candles set in flowers, dried botanicals, or found objects. I like beeswax candles because they drip less, but I still use bobeches, which are circular glass or marble pieces that fit between the candle and candlestick to catch dripping wax.

I also enjoy using candle shades. When my shop first opened, we imported them from England, where they have been used for centuries. They shed soft light, eliminating glare. Use dripless candles and click the shade and liner securely into the metal carrier before placing it on the candle. Leaving shaded candles in

ABOVE RIGHT: A seating chart for a Sweet Sixteen party. The name cards can be moved around to make the best seating plan possible.
BELOW: These luxurious place and menu cards are richly embossed with elegant designs.

ABOVE: Here is what you will need for decorating a candle shade. I have chosen the most perfect smalley leaves to use and will glue them, overlapping, one at a time. Galax leaves are also an option.
BELOW LEFT: This shade is decorated with fuchsia smalley leaves and set on a metal carrier that slips onto the candle. It would look beautiful on a table set with roses and lots of glistening glass.
BELOW RIGHT: Dried rose petals are glued to this shade on a porcelain lamp, casting a flattering light.

drafts or unattended when lit could be a fire hazard. You can buy a wardrobe of candle shades for your table or decorate your own.

Petal Candle Shade

Flat leaves or petals, such as smalley (shown here), magnolia, galax, or lemon leaves; or petals from roses or peonies
Candle shade with a protective liner and companion carrier
Hot glue gun

1. Select leaves that are the same size; reserve smaller ones for later use.
2. Starting at the bottom, glue the leaves onto the candle shade, working your way around row by row. Glue each row overlapping the previous one, so that none of the shade shows.
3. Use the smaller leaves to fill in around the edges, placing them under and over the previous row as needed.

A word here about scent. I still love using fragrant candles. I use our own Cherchez's Field Flower candles all around the house, especially in living areas. As people walk through our front door, the scent is as welcoming as a warm hug. However, I think fragrance at the table can be problematic. As Victorian tastemaker Mrs. Beeton said in the 1870s,

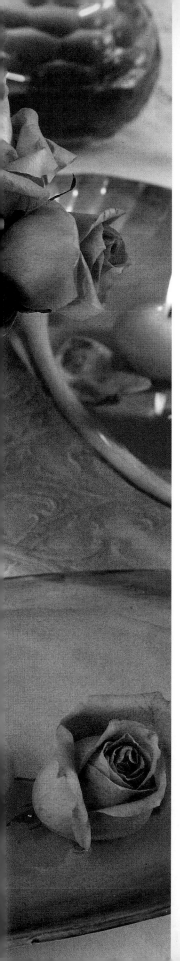

"To some, the perfume of such flowers as gardenias, stephanotis, hyacinths is not offensive, but to others, the strong scent in a heated room, especially during dinner, is considered very unpleasant." Heavy scent can overwhelm the joy of savoring the taste and scent of food, so make careful choices.

Here are some suggestions for using candles more effectively:

- To make candles burn more evenly and slowly, wrap them in foil and place them in the refrigerator for several hours before they are to be lit.
- Always trim wicks to ¼ inch.
- Pour excess wax off candles.
- Store candles flat in a cool place to prevent warping.
- Never leave lit candles unattended.
- Discard candles when they get to within several inches of the holder or the decorations surrounding them.

Finger bowls were in common use up until the turn of the century. I have old housekeeping books that show cut-glass bowls with all types of flowers floating in them. Before they went out of fashion, these bowls were as much a part of the table setting as a knife and fork. Today, we use them on more formal occasions or

LEFT: These antique Wedgwood pieces are among my favorites. The Nautilus shell holds grapes and roses. Candles and petals float in mussel dishes. Scallop shells serve as dessert plates and there are even shell butter pats.

RIGHT, TOP: For individual place settings, hollow out an artichoke and insert a short candle. Place in a clay pot and tie with a ribbon.

SECOND FROM TOP: I showed dried flower candle rings in my book *The Scented Room*. They can be used from year to year if stored properly.

THIRD FROM TOP: I inserted a candle in this clay pot and filled in the base all around it with pink pepper berries and fresh rose heads.

BOTTOM: Put a pillar candle in a hurricane lamp and fill the space around it with colorful shells.

Rose

when one of the courses is a finger food. The finger bowl should be half filled with cool water unless it is being used after something informal, like lobster, then the water should be warm.

Whenever I'm in Florence, I always buy rosewater to use in finger bowls, at the Farmacia di Santa Maria Novella. It's located in a seventeenth-century convent and has been open continuously since then. The pale aqua label on the bottle is evocative of the Renaissance and is just as beautiful as the Farmacia. You can make your own rosewater by using this recipe and adding essence of rose or rose geranium oil.

Floral Finger Bowls

This makes enough for about six medium-size finger bowls.

4 cups distilled water
6 drops floral essential oil
6 freshly picked whole flower
heads or blossoms

1. Boil the water. Add the essential oil of your choice—rose, lavender, or violet is nice—and set aside to cool.
2. When cool, fill each finger bowl halfway with the scented water. Just before guests arrive, add some flowers to each finger bowl. Use small ones like roses, gardenias, mock orange, nasturtiums, sweet peas, or violets and well-shaped leaves from plants like ivy.
3. Place a bowl at each setting when you serve dessert.

TOP LEFT: I'm always on the lookout for attractive glass bowls, for which I have many uses, including finger bowls. Float small flowers in them, like the rose here, with the rose geranium leaf next to it.

LEFT: Transparent organza ribbons swirl over this lacy table set with elegant china. The gift favor and nosegay on either side of the crescent salad dish will be tokens of a wonderful party.

In *Nancy Lancaster, Her Life, Her Work, Her Art,* Ms. Lancaster explains that she has always been in search of beauty, and comments on the elusiveness of what creates it. Then she tells about visiting an old lady from a fine family who had some lovely china on display. She writes, "She kept the china in a cupboard, and around the handle on one soup terrine she had tied a pink ribbon. That's what I loved. This lady thought that very beautiful, decorating her greatest prize with a pink taffeta ribbon." I love the picture this story evokes.

Collecting old ribbons, along with old textiles and lace, is a hobby, and in my book *Simply Flowers* I talked about them at length. Flowers can be wonderfully enhanced by these trimmings, so look for unusual ribbons, like wired or embroidered ones. I have found fine, pretty, old ribbons at tag sales where they've been tucked into old sewing baskets. Remember that they are an important complement, but they should not overpower the flowers.

At the table, ribbons can be used in lots of charming ways: hung from chandeliers and candelabra, tied onto napkins and party favors, encircling vases, and draped around chairs. As with all the ideas in this chapter, you are only limited by your imagination.

TOP RIGHT: Because I was born in May, and my twin niece and nephew were born on May 1, I always look forward to May Day. It's the day that celebrates the coming of spring. Historically, Maypoles are tied at the top with long ribbons, which children hold and dance around. Here, ribbons are tied from the center of a Victorian flower ball made of fresh bouvardia, lilacs, tulips, stocks, and roses and then softly drawn to the finials of each chair.

RIGHT: A bouquet of graceful flowers and ivy is secured to each finial with wide ribbons. Decorating the chairs like this with flowers, leaves, and ribbons creates an entire flower oasis within the room. Ivy encircles dishes and napkins.

🦋 LEFT: The center of
this table is decorated with
groupings of various small
vases and deep blue votive
candleholders. Silver
mint julep cups are filled
to overflowing with
all-white flowers, while
bigger vases hold the
taller calla lilies.
FOLLOWING PAGE: Consider
using small vases like
these, which have a
charm all their own. Little
cups, miniature teapots,
and delicate antique
baskets look so
enchanting with individual
flowers like roses and
pansies in them.
DETAIL: I like to use
ironstone pitchers for
iced tea, milk, water,
and, of course, flowers
like these hydrangeas.

Choosing Containers

baskets • bowls • vases • cachepots

"When all the guests can see each other, the feeling of cheerful good fellowship is unrestricted." Gertrude Jeykll said this in her book *Flower Decoration,* published in 1907, and it's still true today. Choosing the correct container for the centerpiece is critical for many reasons, and making sure your guests see and interact with one another is one of them. The height and proportion of the container will determine how tall or wide the centerpiece can be, and how easily conversation can be carried on around it.

The relationship of the centerpiece to the table is important, so I think it's always a good idea to try the container in the center of the table before you start adding the flowers: It's easier to see the space you want to fill that way. Use your own good judgment. For example, if I'm having six instead of the eight people my table will comfortably hold, I allow my centerpiece to take up more room.

Generally speaking, centerpieces for the table should come to either below or above eye level. Using low containers is usually best, I find. If you plan on using a tall vase or a topiary, make sure it is slender and that your guests can still see one another across the table. Larger vases can be used when the table is very large and long, since in that case, guests will be speaking to the people on either side rather than across from them.

Remember that at the table, the flowers and vase will be seen close up and from every angle. This means that special attention should be paid to choosing a container that harmonizes with the tableware you will use and also relates to the flowers. Tableware, vase, flowers—they make a total picture.

Start with color, which is the most important tool you have. Use it to your advantage to create punch and eye appeal. I've learned a lot about color from reading Constance Spry, the English gardener and floral designer whose books hold a special place on my shelves. Though the photographs in them may be dated, what she has to say is not. Her remarks are instructional and pithy, as when she describes putting a bunch of vivid red geraniums in a brilliant green malachite vase because "they have something to say to each other." This illustrates the options you have when color-coordinating your containers and flowers, so use your imagination; you will be surprised at the possibilities.

31

🦋 ABOVE: A peek at a shelf in our kitchen, which holds some favorite vases. When I come in from the garden with an armful of flowers, it's fun matching them up with a container that will make them look even better—if possible! These vases have been accumulated over years from antiques shows, flea markets, and tag sales.

Constance Spry also said that "judging by the number of people who complain that they never have the right vase at the right moment, there must be plenty of vase cupboards which need replenishing!" It's fun to collect containers. It can be done inexpensively, because so many forgotten objects make great flower holders—they just have to hold water. A short list would include soup tureens, sugar bowls, brandy snifters, fruit compotes, silver bowls and beakers, salad and finger bowls, wine tubs and coolers, jardinieres, cachepots, urns, baskets, and trays. Look in your closets with a fresh eye. When visiting your parents and relatives, peek in their attics and basements, and always brake for tag sales—you may find some treasures.

🦋 BELOW LEFT: The container you decide to use is determined by several factors, but it should be appropriate to the flowers it will hold. I like using cans as vases, especially with casual summer flowers like snapdragons. BELOW: The shape of this rare two-tiered glass vase is ideal for the table, as guests are able to see through it.

Your container and the flowers in it should be appropriate to the occasion and to each other. Look at the flowers, their colors and shapes. Once put into a container, the two become one. Although I dislike centerpieces that are overworked and pretentious, this certainly doesn't mean that I never use an ornate or valuable container. Just remember that the arrangement should be suitable. Some of the prettiest flowers I've seen were arranged in modest containers, like moldy old clay flowerpots or charming baskets.

The table is a stage, allowing us to be creative in a less serious way. Because of the temporary role of flowers—as decoration for the duration of dinner—you should feel free to experiment. One way I

do this is by using multiple vases, which makes for an interesting effect. Try repeating the same ordinary shape, like the colored teapots shown in this chapter or a collection of silver trumpet vases of various designs and sizes.

Another idea is to hollow out fruits and vegetables like melons, peppers, coconuts, and artichokes and use them as flower containers. In this case, choose one type of flower in a single color to coordinate with the fruits and vegetables you are putting them in.

Try clustering small containers like cordial glasses, baby or christening cups, small pitchers, miniature baskets, and silver beakers. Putting one in front of each place setting gives an intimate feeling. Small containers also look great bunched in the center of the table as a focal point, and a long table can be enhanced by using many small containers scattered among candles and other table accessories. Almost any well-shaped blossom looks best in these tiny receptacles, which should be filled to overflowing with flowers that have had their stems cut short.

Containers for centerpieces can come

🦋 LEFT, TOP: Clustering more than one vase, especially if you have several of the same shape, makes for an interesting centerpiece. These vividly colored teapots are the ideal foil for bright spring flowers: daffodils, tulips, and irises.

SECOND FROM TOP: Don't underestimate small containers. Here, silver christening and baby cups are massed on top of a wood table, where the flowers can be seen close up. The stems of the roses were clipped short.

THIRD FROM TOP: Shallow bowls usually look comfortable in the center of the table. This Victorian salad bowl, a cabbage shape, holds a fall favorite—flowering kale. The elegance of the silver works with the common earthiness of the kale.

BOTTOM: Tall flower arrangements work on the table as long as guests can see through them to talk to one another. For example, these tall, papery poppies, though oversized, seem to float delicately out of a green cut-glass vase.

4 Classic Containers

I never worry about last-minute dinner guests. I always do a simple centerpiece using one of my favorite containers, which gives me time to look forward to my company.

🐝 ABOVE: This 7-inch silver bowl was a wedding present. It was so formal, I wondered what I would do with it. I found it was perfect for potpourri and for flowers like these saucy daisies, their stems cut short and nestled into a piece of floral foam.

🐝 BELOW: An old wire jardiniere is the right size for a potted plant. This ivy topiary looks good tucked into the moss lining the space between wire and pot. I prefer using plants when eating outside in our garden. Fussy flowers seem redundant.

🐝 ABOVE: On a trip to France we visited a cooperative that makes baskets for every business from laundries to bakeries. This souvenir is perfect for fruit, frequently twelve green apples whose fresh scent creates a relaxed mood at the table.

🐝 BELOW: Tag sales are a source of great finds: This old plant holder with worn paint was just right, as far as I was concerned. When I got it home, my dried hydrangeas coordinated beautifully, as if I'd had a petal in my pocket to match it.

ABOVE: You will need the following items when making your leaf vases: a hot glue gun, glass tumblers, clay pots, rubber bands, flat leaves like red and green magnolias, and pretty ribbons and trims.

in any material imaginable: silver, brass, glass, or china—the list is endless. Create your own vases by covering glass tumblers or little clay pots with such leaves as magnolia, mountain laurel, oak, or bay. Tropical leaves can be overlapped and tied onto big vases. This is a simple idea and gives the table an unexpected look.

There are two other points to consider. First, all porous receptacles such as baskets or unglazed pots must be lined so they can hold water. Some people have tin liners custom-made for this purpose. I find it handy to use glass jars, recycled plastic containers, or, if a basket is shallow, aluminum pie tins as liners, along with aluminum foil.

Also remember that a poorly cleaned container can foster the growth of bacteria, shortening the life of your flowers. So after using it, rinse each container with a little household bleach and then dry it thoroughly.

FAR LEFT: Individual leaf vases are easy to make and give flowers a lift. Here, large oak leaves surround a bouquet of dried apricot roses tied with a wire ribbon.

CENTER: Bay leaves are glued to a simple clay pot. You can put wheat, flowers, or even candy in it. Here, a Styrofoam ball is covered with moss and wrapped in gold trim.

NEAR LEFT: Treated magnolia leaves like this come in dark green and red. They are glued to a small glass tumbler, which is then filled with tulips. Silk twine is tied around the middle.

Making Leaf Vases

Oak or Magnolia Leaves

Oak or Magnolia leaves
Hot glue gun
Glass tumbler
Rubber band
Silk cords or ribbon

1. Press leaves between heavy books for several days to dry.
2. With a hot glue gun, attach the leaves overlapping each other all around the tumbler.
3. Secure at center with rubber band and lean on side while glue dries.
4. Trim leaves on bottom flush with the glass.
5. Tie around middle with silk cord or wired ribbon.
6. Fill with fresh or dried flowers.

Bay Leaves

Bay leaves
Hot glue gun
Rimless clay pot
Styrofoam ball
Sheet moss
Metallic trims
  and ribbons

1. Soak bay leaves overnight so they will be flexible. Pat dry before using.
2. With a glue gun, attach leaves, row by row, overlapping, top to bottom.
3. Use a Styrofoam ball that will just sit on the rim of the pot. Cover it with sheet moss applied with the glue gun.
4. Tie with metallic trims and ribbons. You can also fill these pots with dried flowers or a little plant.

Chapter 4

🐦 LEFT: All the
elements on the table
should coordinate to
create a lovely effect.
A turquoise and pink
tablecloth gave
me an opportunity
to use the French
opaline-glass vase,
compote and service
plates. Old-fashioned
roses and peonies
complete the picture.
FOLLOWING PAGE: Mixing
flowers of different textures
is a nice way to create a
centerpiece. Here, dried
hydrangeas, roses, and
gardenias fill a silver basket
to overflowing.
The fake peach is an
unexpected touch.
DETAIL: Sometimes all you
need to cheer up a table
is a single gerbera daisy
in a simple glass vase.

Creating Centerpieces

flowers ❦ foliage ❦ fruits ❦ topiaries

"First flowers on the table; then food." I was so pleased to come across this old Danish proverb recently, as I've always enjoyed decorating the table more than cooking the meal. I used to feel guilty about this, especially when I was first married. Food was supposed to be the focus, and in order to qualify for the "ideal wife" club, you had to aspire to be a gourmet cook. This in addition to being a working executive!

I've always preferred using simple recipes with fresh, seasonal ingredients and then spending what extra time I have fussing with the flowers. But since reading that even a genius like Monet could say, "I am not good at anything, but painting and gardening," I no longer make excuses. Decorating the table is the thing I do best and enjoy most. And what I like to focus on is the centerpiece.

Creating something beautiful for the table should be fun, yet many people dread it. They don't feel they are creative enough. I disagree. Although some seem to have a knack for doing everything with superb style, most of us can get good results if we just try. By working with flowers over and over again, we start to develop our own style—and self-confidence. But since the subject of creating centerpieces is a big and, sometimes, confusing one, I will break it down into bite-size pieces.

Flower arrangements should always look fresh and spontaneous, not overworked and the flowers should look as if they were just brought in from the garden. The first thing to consider in working with them has to be **color.** It can make or break your total presentation.

Use color as your organizing principle. The choices here are personal, so use your favorites. Don't overlook the impact of using a single color. All-white flowers always look great and are easy to find throughout the year. Here's a list of my favorite monochromatic groupings:

White: freesia, hydrangea, lilac, lily, lisianthus, petunia, Queen Anne's lace, rose, tulip, daisy, lily-of-the-valley.

Pink/Peach: carnation, foxglove, gerbera, peony, poppy, ranunculus, rose, snapdragon, sweet pea, dahlia.

Blue/Purple: anemone, bellflower, cornflower, pansy, delphinium, hyacinth, iris, lavender, lilac, clematis.

Yellow/Orange: calendula, coreopsis, daffodil, nasturtium, pansy, sunflower, tansy, tulip, yarrow, zinnia.

41

🦋 Above Left: Bright yellow lemon slices and roses fill a glass bowl. Center: Radiant red cranberries and roses come together in a small glass vase. Right: Kumquats support purple irises in a cylinder vase.

Visible Flowers—Invisible Vases

Something different comes from filling or wrapping a simple glass vase with the unexpected. Make these the same day you will be using them. Flowers don't last as long when they share the same water with fruit.

Lemons and Roses

1. Cut floral foam to fit into the bottom of a straight-sided bowl, leaving a ¼-inch space between it and the sides.
2. Cut lemon slices ¼ inch wide and wedge into the sides of the bowl, overlapping each other.
3. Push cut roses into foam and add some water.

Cranberries and Roses

1. Fill the vase to about halfway with cranberries.
2. Place roses in center, adding cranberries all around to support the flowers.
3. Add water and tie the neck of the vase with a flat iris leaf.

Kumquats and Irises

1. Put a rubber band 1 inch from the bottom of the irises and put in vase.
2. Add one kumquat at a time all the way around, pushing them down.
3. When vase is filled, add water.
4. Add short irises if desired.

Marbles and Daffodils

1. Cut straight-stemmed flowers so heads extend 1 inch above top of vase.
2. Fill half of the vase with the clear glass marbles.
3. Holding stems tightly together, add your flowers.
4. Add more marbles all around for support, then add water.

Asparagus and Anemones

1. Stand the asparagus stalks around the outside of a recycled can, holding them in place with a rubber band.
2. Tie ribbon to cover rubber band.
3. Add anemones, then add water.

Wheat and Dried Flowers

1. Stand the stalks of wheat around a recycled can, holding them in place with a rubber band.
2. Tie raffia over rubber band in a bow.
3. Fill can with dried material like sunflowers, poppy heads, and yarrow.

Leaves also add color, from grays to greens. They can bring texture to a flower arrangement or can be used alone very effectively. I often use ivy, euphorbia, laurel, and rhododendron, among others.

Regarding strongly scented flowers at the table, as I said in Chapter 2, I recommend discretion when using them.

The next point to consider is that your centerpiece should be in **proportion** to the size of your table—neither too small nor too large. It should be below eye level, so people can talk to one another easily.

In her book *Recipes for Successful Dining,* Elsie De Wolfe stressed the importance of keeping "your table decorations low, low, low." In order to make these low arrangements, you must not be afraid to cut the stems short. In many cases, the flowers will look dramatically different—usually better, I've found.

Composition throws most people off. There are no set rules. Here, however, are a few important suggestions.

• Buy or pick more flowers than you think you will need. Your arrangement should be full, and if you use an abundance of materials, the result will be twice as effective as a skimpy offering. Decorate other rooms in your home with any surplus.

BELOW LEFT: Brilliant daffodils surrounded by transparent marbles in a vase. CENTER: Fresh asparagus create a unique container for anemones. RIGHT: The same concept works for dried wheats and flowers.

Summer zinnias in colorful 1920s pottery mixing bowls parade down the center of this wonderful old green painted table. Vintage dishcloths serve as napkins and a rag mat cushions the bowl in the center.

Small Is Sublime

Experiment with using individual bouquets at each place setting. Small containers filled with lush, little assortments of flowers always give the table a personal feeling.

🐝 ABOVE: A miniature watering can that was a Christmas ornament is used as a container. The casual mood of the summer blossoms complements the straw mats and pottery dishes.

🐝 BELOW: Make this rose-in-a-pot in advance, then add fresh leaves at the last minute. Choose a 3-inch pot with character and fill it with a piece of floral foam. Then insert a freeze-dried rose.

🐝 ABOVE: Gather some silver cups and fill them with gifts from the garden: roses, snapdragons, and morning glories. These bouquets make lovely presents when tucked into little pots.

🐝 BELOW: A favorite miniature porcelain cabbage, without its cover, becomes a perfect place to set a bunch of bright orange nasturtiums. They match the floral pattern in the vintage tablecloth.

- Whatever is used in the centerpiece must be impeccable, as fresh as possible and without blemishes. Your guests will be looking at them close up all through the meal.
- To make the table look fuller, place flowers at individual settings in lieu of or in addition to your centerpiece. These are less expensive, as the smaller containers hold fewer flowers, and they take less time to make.
- To look more natural, flower heads should not be inserted all facing in one direction. By the same token, they should be recessed at different heights, rather than the same height. This will give dimension to your centerpiece and it won't look like a pincushion.
- Use flowers at every stage of maturity, from bud to full bloom, for variety.
- Use large flowers or leaves, such as hydrangeas, as a base. Then add smaller flowers as accents.
- Flowers should not be a status symbol. Approach all flowers equally and use what you like. Combine the familiar with the exotic; use wild and cultivated; coordinate fresh with dried.
- Know when to stop. The more you fuss, the less natural your flowers will look.

OPPOSITE: Foliage is rarely used alone in centerpieces, which is unfortunate, as it can be quite magnificent. Using leaves can produce results like this glass vase of glorious ruby chard. The pomegranates and red tole tray accentuate the brilliant red veins in the leaves and, of course, the stems.

RIGHT, TOP: Look around for usable foliage like these delicate morning glory vines. They look like they are actually growing from the porcelain blossom that will bloom forever.

CENTER: Dutchman's pipe is a wonderful old-fashioned climber that you often see growing on farmhouses. Here it surrounds a dinner plate.

BOTTOM: Herbs are wonderful to use on the table—herbs of various colors and textures, when tucked into a miniature trug, make a special place setting. Snips of pineapple mint, lamb's ears, angelica, sage, and scented geranium are included.

Henry David Thoreau said, "Live each season as it passes: Breathe the air, drink the drink, taste the fruit, and resign yourself to the influences of each." Our tables should reflect the rhythm of the seasons. Although these days almost everything is available, we should look forward to the changes each season brings. Using dried materials in the fall is almost a relief after summer's bounty.

Fruits and vegetables lend themselves naturally to low arrangements on the table and always look lush when arranged alone or with flowers. The shapes are interesting and the colors are varied and sometimes unexpected. The other day I saw a display of white eggplants at the market and thought how beautiful they would look mixed with mushrooms and a cauliflower in a basket lined with ruffled green cabbage leaves.

When working with fruits and vegetables, remember to select different sizes and shapes. A walk through any farmers' market will illustrate the varieties available. Line your baskets and containers with leaves like hosta, ivy, magnolia, pittosporum, or galax. Seasonal offerings are inspirational—and delicious. Here is a list of fruits and vegetables that I enjoy using, organized by color:

Red: apple, currant, grape, peach, pepper, plum, pomegranate, radish, raspberry, strawberry, tomato.
Orange: gourd, kumquat, orange, pepper, persimmon, tangerine, orange.

ABOVE LEFT: Emily Post said that "bread is like dresses, hats and shoes—in other words, essential." Especially when you can use it in centerpieces, like this one of dinner rolls, leaves, and chilies.
LEFT: This hardy peasant bread was so attractive that I used it with colorful peppers as the table decoration for an informal supper.
OPPOSITE: I'm a tomato lover, and each summer I look forward to eating and arranging them. Here, a big cabbage is hollowed out and filled with the several delicious varieties growing in our garden.

Purple: red cabbage, cherry, eggplant, fig, grape, onion, pepper, plum, radicchio.

Yellow: banana, grapefruit, lemon, peach, pepper, pineapple, summer squash.

White: cauliflower, gourd, mushroom, onion, squash.

Green: apple, artichoke, avocado, broccoli, celery, fennel, fig, gooseberry, grape, kale, lime, pepper, squash.

If you love to bake or have a good bakery nearby, try using bread in a table still life. This is a nice winter idea because afterward you have a ready-made picnic for the birds. Other food—like cakes, chocolates, cookies, olives, or even pickles—can also be used in centerpieces.

How about using some choices we might not readily think of, including seashells, rocks and minerals, antique porcelain flowers, silver animals and birds, terra-cotta fruits and vegetables—even your young children's colorful arts and crafts projects.

Crystallized fruits and flowers add a sophisticated touch to desserts like sorbet, ice cream, or simple cakes. Filling glass compotes with fruits and berries makes for an edible centerpiece that always looks elegant.

🦋 OPPOSITE: Keep your themes simple when doing centerpieces with vegetables—let the textures, colors, and shapes carry the day. An old melon basket filled with seasonal produce looks great. I used a favorite—hyacinth bean vines—to twist around the handle. The flowers turn into vivid purple pods later in the season.

ABOVE RIGHT: Gourds are hardy and easy to grow but they take a lot of room. Last year I bought these all-white ones at our local farmers' market. They look handsome with the different varieties of green-and-white squash and a small watermelon. Straw flowers add a dash of yellow.

RIGHT: The focal point of this outdoor buffet is the vivid purples of the peppers, eggplant, cabbage, opal basil, and hyacinth beans, complemented by the deep blue bowl and plates.

ABOVE: There are so many glorious ways to combine flowers and fruits or vegetables in centerpieces. Grapes always make a suitable background and are available year-round. Here blush roses are combined with coxcomb, geranium, and sedum nestled in a rustic basket surrounded by blackberry leaves.

BELOW: If you haven't tried making frosted or crystallized fruits, you could start with small berries and grapes. All you'll need besides the fresh, firm fruit is granulated sugar and egg whites.

OPPOSITE: This handsome compote is an old one from Austria. The top three dishes hold freshly frosted strawberries and two types of grapes. The bottom bowl is filled with pomegranates and pears.

You can use little flowers, such as violets, pansies, or nasturtium blossoms; rose petals; berries, like blueberries, strawberries, gooseberries, or currants; small fruits, like grapes, lemons, kumquats, or lady apples; and the leaves from edible herbs.

Frosting Fruits and Flowers

Your choice of flowers or fruit
Finely granulated sugar
Egg whites

1. Wash flowers or fruit.

2. Gently pat dry.

3. Pour the sugar into one bowl and beat the egg whites until frothy in another.

4. Using a pastry brush, apply a thin coat of egg white to the flowers or fruit.

5. Sprinkle with the sugar, being sure to cover all sides adequately.

6. Set on a cookie sheet or wire rack for several hours to dry. Then arrange.

7. Rose petals and violets can be layered in wax paper for up to a week.

I also like to use fresh or dried topiaries. These miniature trees always look elegant, with their classic sculptured

🦋 ABOVE: A forest of topiaries set on a sideboard. I like using them on tabletops because, like these examples in shades of green-tufted moss, they always look graceful and elegant but not overdone.

BELOW: Here are some of the supplies you will need in order to make a topiary: Sahara floral foam, a sharp knife, sheet moss, flowerpots, dowels, and dried flower heads and greens.

shapes, and even though they are not low, they are slender enough for guests to see around or through. I especially like fresh ones of English ivy, lavender, rosemary, or myrtle clipped into neat forms.

Dried topiaries are always nice in a room and can serve as effective centerpieces. Last year I made four amusing ones out of dried materials, one for each season of the year. You can use almost any dried botanical you have available.

How to Make a Four-Seasons Topiary

Sahara floral foam
Flowerpot
Dowel for trunk
Styrofoam ball
Hot glue gun
Botanical materials of your
  choice
Sheet moss
Ribbon and trims

1. Carve Sahara to fit into the flowerpot, then firmly press it in.
2. Insert one end of dowel into Styrofoam ball and the other end securely into the Sahara in the pot.
3. Glue botanicals to the Styrofoam ball, covering completely.
4. Add the sheet moss at the base, covering the top of the foam.
5. Cover the dowel to look like a tree trunk or paint it.
6. Decorate pots with ribbons and coverings like fabric or foil.

🦋 ABOVE: This "spring" topiary features dried roses accentuated with pink pepperberries, all wrapped in fuchsia tulle and silk ribbon.

🦋 BELOW: The "fall" topiary is made from a selection of nuts. Wheat sheaves and a wide wired ribbon encircle the trunk.

🦋 ABOVE: Zinnias and sheet moss cover the "summer" topiary, and thatchy green string ties up a weathered flowerpot.

🦋 BELOW: Icy silver tones proclaim "winter" in this topiary decorated with metallic stars, ribbon, and shiny foil wrapping.

We all want our flowers to last as long as possible. This will depend on how you select and condition them. Here are some things to remember:

- When gathering flowers, the best time to cut them is in the early morning, when the stems contain the most moisture. Then place them *immediately* in water. If you can, cut them the day before they are needed and place them in a cool place in deep, water-filled containers so they get a long drink.
- Always use a sharp knife or florist shears and cut the stems cleanly on a slant to maximize the amount of water they can absorb. Do not use scissors—they pinch the stems closed.
- When choosing flowers to cut or buy, look for flower heads that are firm and crisp-looking. Do not use if the petals are bruised, the heads are drooping, or the pollen has built up. Leaves should not be wilted or discolored. Stems should be strong, not spongy.

What you do to your flowers once you get them inside will determine how long they last. This is called **conditioning.** What you want to do is to get water flowing up the stem to the flower at the top. To do this:

- Remove foliage and clip off thorns. Any leaves in the water will rot, shortening the life of the flowers.
- Cut the tips of all the stems on a slant *again,* but this time under water. This prevents air bubbles from forming.
- Flowers with woody stems like lilacs and magnolia need to have the tips of their stems crushed gently with a hammer. You can also make a two-inch vertical cut up the stem with a knife and scrape off several inches at the tip.
- Flowers with hollow stems like lupin and delphinium can be up-ended, filled with water, and then the stem plugged with a piece of cotton.
- Flowers with milky sap like hollyhocks and poppies should be cauterized by holding the end of the stem over a candle until it turns black. This prevents the sap from blocking the intake of water.
- If you have tulips with bent stems or roses with droopy flower heads, roll them tightly in newspaper, then stand them overnight up to their necks in a bucket of cold water. Prick droopy tulips, roses, and ranunculus just under the flower head with a straight pin. This releases trapped air.
- Wilting flowers can be revived by using one of three tricks. The simplest is to cut the stems frequently. You can also put them in several inches of boiling hot water for a minute or two. If you have tired-looking flowers, especially violets, roses, or gardenias, they can usually be perked up by being immersed *entirely* in cool water in the tub or sink for up to fifteen minutes.

After the meal, you will want to continue enjoying your flowers. Flowers are living things, so don't neglect them. Check the water level *daily* and keep the vase filled to the top with cool water.

You don't have to remove flowers from their vase to change the water. Put the vase in the sink and flush out the old water, refilling it with fresh.

Spray leaves and flowers, which absorb moisture, with a mister. If it is dry in the room, use a humidifier.

If you wish to keep the water and flowers in your arrangement as fresh as possible, adding a commercial flower food to the water is usually the easiest method. It inhibits bacteria and encourages flowers to open and last longer.

Another option is to add one of the following to the water: a few drops of household bleach to get rid of stagnant odors and kill bacteria; a piece of absorbent charcoal to clear up cloudiness or bad odors; an aspirin to retard bacteria and limit moisture loss; or a little sugar or lemonade to move the moisture up through the stems.

🦋 ABOVE: Here are the tools and supplies you'll need to create centerpieces. Upper left are two sizes of hot glue guns with glue sticks for dried flower and craft projects. Next are two underwater stem cutters. When you push the flower into them, the stem ends are automatically cut on a slant under the water. The little packets and the larger container are filled with commercial flower food. My favorite cutting tools are in a row, left to right: good-quality pruning shears for snipping woody branches; "hold and cut" shears for cutting flowers with thorns; garden scissors, which I use most frequently; and a sharp folding knife for scraping stems and cutting blocks of foam.

🦋 BELOW: Here are some things that you may want to use to anchor flowers when arranging them. Left to right: Crumpled, flexible chicken wire can be used to position large masses of flowers. Polished pebbles and marbles are attractive when used in clear vases. The green ceramic frog and other flower holders made from metal mesh or pins come in handy when using bowls and baskets. I use waterproof tape to make a grid atop vases, a useful trick for holding flowers in place. The tape and floral adhesive also secure flower holders to the bottom of their containers. Blocks of floral foam complete the picture: The green water-absorbent, Oasis, is for fresh flowers, and the brown, Sahara, is for dried ones.

Chapter
5

LEFT: Seasonal offerings usually make sensational table presentations. The stone cupid holding a nosegay to his heart symbolizes summer, as do the luscious roses that were just gathered in the garden outside.

FOLLOWING PAGE: A clutch of the first spring daffodils brightens a breakfast table set with handicrafts from our town's annual church bazaar. Duck place mats and hand-knit poached egg warmers add a touch of whimsy to the start of the day.

DETAIL: A graceful nineteenth-century chair in black with distinctive gold stenciling of flowers and foliage.

Setting Tables Inside

kitchen • dining room • library • buffets

"Even if it is but once a week, we must gather at the table, alone or with friends or with lots of friends or with one friend, and eat a meal together. We know that without food we would die. Without fellowship life is not worth living."

Laurie Colwin wrote these lines that capture the essence of the joys of the table. Every so often I curl up with one of her books, usually *Home Cooking* or *More Home Cooking,* where I always find something to make me think—and smile.

Sharing food is the basis for so much of our social life, and nowadays, whether it's for breakfast, lunch, or dinner, we eat meals in every part of the house, from the kitchen table to trays in the bedroom.

Actually, dining rooms didn't exist before the seventeenth century. Before that time, families, servants, and friends ate together in multipurpose halls. Only gradually did people begin to take their meals in more private surroundings.

By the eighteenth century, parlors or bed-sitting-rooms were transformed into dining rooms. For the first time, dining tables and matching chairs became permanent fixtures. These tables were covered with luxurious damask and set with all kinds of magnificent silver.

As a result, by the Victorian era tabletops were crowded with flower epergnes and vases, wineglasses, cutlery, and napkins. A family of even modest means could serve as many as fourteen dishes at a small dinner party. Although the way our tabletops look today have certainly changed, they have nonetheless evolved from those tables of long ago.

Reminiscing about the glorious days on an English country estate before World War I, Nancy Lancaster said, "One had all sorts of dining rooms in those days. The children had their own dining room, the housekeeper had hers, the staff had their hall and we had two of our own." Few people have two dining rooms today, yet we want the rooms in which we dine and socialize to be warm and inviting—even if it's only a breakfast nook.

When you invite someone to your home, you are in charge of their happiness. When I am having guests, my first concern is creating a generous, welcoming atmosphere, which I try to do in many little ways. I start with our front door, decorated with a door bouquet of fresh flowers or a wreath. In autumn, I fill a basket by the door with pumpkins, gourds, and wheat sheaves. Both say "Please come in."

🦋 ABOVE: I enjoy having my dearest friends over for lunch, and although we all have busy schedules, the imminent arrival of spring is always a good excuse to get together. A large heather topiary is set amid colorful primroses and little gifts of my favorite chocolates in attractive boxes with topiaries on them.

🦋 BOTTOM: A friend set this sweet table with her children's artwork. She kept the tableware simple and added a pot of impatiens to an enchanting collection of pastel sculptures and dishes made in art classes and summer camp. It's a lovely reminder, to parents and guests, of how creative children are.

🦋 OPPOSITE: "A simple enough pleasure, surely, to have breakfast alone with one's husband, but how seldom married people in the midst of life achieve it," said Anne Morrow Lindbergh. Morning light filters in on this cozy breakfast table. Fresh linens and china harmonize with the languid wisteria and lupines.

The front hall is the transition from outside to in. This is where I have a large bowl of potpourri. The fragrance lingers while guests are welcomed and coats are hung. It sets a mood as people move into the house in anticipation.

The rest of your house should also set the stage for what is to come. Fireplaces should be lit, furniture gleaming and arranged for ease of conversation. Special soaps, room sprays, and stacks of small towels should be set out in guest powder rooms. This gracious style should continue right into the dining areas, whether they are formal or relaxed. Here is where details make all the difference. Plates should be gently warmed before serving, tableware should be sparkling and napkins oversized, and the centerpiece should be fresh.

Virginia Woolf once said, "One cannot think well, love well, sleep well, if one has not dined well." To create this atmosphere, think about several things:

Good **lighting** in your dining areas will make the food look delicious, the flowers look luxurious, and the guests look attractive. Billy Baldwin, the renowned interior designer, said, "In the dining room the primary source of light should not be, as so many people assume, the chandelier." To create a mood at night, use lots of candles; chandeliers should be dimmed and consider candle sconces on walls for indirect lighting. Rehearse your

ABOVE LEFT: These elegant lilies in glass bottles illustrate how tall but slender flowers can work beautifully on the table.

LEFT: Our friends love Italy, and when they return from their latest trip, they enjoy sharing it with all of us. A map of Rome serves as the cloth. Faience plates, and souvenirs of Rome, Pisa, and Venice decorate a tabletop that will soon be laden with delicious Italian food.

OPPOSITE: Fuchsia tree peonies and lilacs overflow a vase on a table set with antique china and glass. The gray mural and striped seat covers in this library help to create a sophisticated dinner setting.

Cathleen

lighting in advance as colors, including the flowers on your table, will change under artificial light.

Music is essential and adds a special dimension, as it can create a magical background that runs through the entire meal. Remember that it should be appropriate and at a level that will not compete with lively conversation.

Scent in the house matters. Having people over is a great excuse for getting organized. I always polish the furniture with lemon oil. Then I open windows before guests arrive to dispel cooking odors. If it's cool, fireplaces are lit and bundles of lavender or cinnamon sticks smolder. Cherchez room sprays and scented candles are used throughout, although as I mentioned before, I don't care for scent in the dining areas because it competes with the food.

Consider the **comfort** of your guests. The size and shape of the table can affect the conversation and the feeling of congeniality. Each guest should be provided with generous elbow and leg room.

Round or oval tables are usually preferred, but if your table is long and you are only having a small group, don't seat people on the ends.

M. F. K. Fisher said, "Above all, friends should possess the rare gift of sitting!" You want people to linger over a meal, but if the chairs aren't comfortable, they won't. Upholstered chairs look wonderful in a dining room, and you can have pillows made for kitchen chairs.

Everything must be ready by the time your first guest arrives, and the meal must be served on time. Brillat-Savarin in his *La Physiologie du goût* created a set of rules to ensure a perfect meal. One that I love is, "guests are like travelers who aim to arrive at the same destination together."

Consider your own level of comfort. Be sure that you have sufficient assistance with preparing and serving. If you are harried, your guests will sense it. If you don't have the budget for a lavish meal, then edit what you will be serving. It is better to serve a simple meal well than to attempt a more elaborate one imperfectly.

A warm dining room that reflects your tastes and interests is a wonderful place to welcome guests. This distinctive table in its all-white splendor is decorated with cherished objects, including an antique vermeil honeypot filled with a loose bouquet of creamy roses.

The way the table is decorated should be appropriate to the room. The one most people gravitate to for everyday dining is the kitchen, a place that seems warm and inviting in almost any home. Its informal atmosphere make it a place where people enjoy congregating and eating—any child can tell you that. Tables in the kitchen can be casually decorated. Bowls of fruits and vegetables, your children's arts and crafts projects, rustic baskets filled with wildflowers and herbs—all work in relaxed settings for meals.

The dining room is where many of us celebrated special occasions and holiday meals as children. They have gone in and out of fashion over the years, but today survive as places where we entertain in traditional and elegant ways. Because it's a room that exists solely for dining, the table becomes the focus, a miniature stage where you can use your personal taste and style to the fullest. This is your chance to use all your sophisticated objects and antiques as centerpieces—statuary, porcelain flowers, paperweights, figurines, found objects, folk art, polished baskets, silver and vermeil epergnes—to create dramatic focal points on a distinctively appointed table.

Spreading out into other rooms like libraries and living rooms is fun and sometimes necessary if you've invited many people. Even today, in France especially, some people adhere to the old custom of

OPPOSITE: This opulent table is set with objects from around the world: a brass Indian pedestal bowl filled with flowers; ormolu candlesticks draped with beaded bobèches; French St. Louis glass; and a satin appliqué cloth.

ABOVE RIGHT: This tabletop inspired by the Orient is a result of combining brilliant reds and yellows. A polished basket bursts with tropical greens, chrysanthemums, and parrot tulips.

RIGHT: Dinner for two in a contemporary mode, where the focal point is the glass Aalto vase filled with perky anemones. Understated tableware in crisp white completes the picture.

having no dining room, serving guests instead in various salons. Coordinate your table and centerpiece with the colors and furnishings already in the room you are using—nothing could be prettier.

Buffets appeal to many of us. I like them because they give the occasion a feeling of abundance, with a nice combination of food, decorations, and lots of activity. When there are large groups of people expected—family reunions, graduations, or holidays like Thanksgiving or Christmas—buffets are a graceful way to entertain with less help and fuss.

A buffet also has several advantages over a sit-down dinner. Because it's an adaptable event, more guests can be invited, even up to the last minute, and there is no difficulty about latecomers or cancellations. I also seem to be able to spend more time with my guests, being less involved in the mechanics and anxieties that come with serving a multicourse meal.

The word "buffet" means sideboard in French, and that is traditionally where the food is served. A long or round table also works well. A centerpiece for a sideboard placed up against the wall or at the center of a large table can be big and dramatic. Pile flowers, leaves, fruits, and vegetables high. Decorations can lap onto fireplaces and chandeliers too, in addition to the other rooms where people will be seated to eat.

🦋 A table in the living room is usually home to stacks of art books, but it doubles as a dining table for a change of pace. Here are several details:
TOP LEFT: The table is covered with a luxurious antique French quilted cloth, then set with old Meissen dishes, French cutlery, and delicate glass.
CENTER: Amusing wire butterfly napkin rings.
BOTTOM: An unusual centerpiece of an old painted urn nestled in eighteenth-century Lyon silk. The tôle flowers in the urn and antique objects at bottom are part of ongoing collections.
OPPOSITE: A generous French country armchair piled high with soft, silk-covered pillows.

Buffets are versatile and can be set up for any meal, including brunch and desserts. As any English mystery buff (myself included) can tell you, breakfast buffets are a natural. All summer long we have house guests, who want to relax and sleep late. At the start of their stay, I arrange various juices in glass pitchers along with jams and a big fruit salad in the fridge, and I set the timer on the coffee machine. In the mornings, I put everything out on a sideboard already set with a big jug of wildflowers, cutlery, dishes, and a small toaster oven. I add a generous basket of breads. People get up when they like, forage for themselves, and start a leisurely day—no pressure for them or me.

A successful buffet depends on organization, so here are some suggestions:

• Nothing is more frustrating than a line of hungry people moving at a snail's pace. For more than twenty guests, I use a table with both sides offering the same food. Things flow twice as fast.
• If you have room, serve beverages on another table to relieve the crush. If you have the budget, hire a waiter to serve cocktails before and beverages during the meal. Guests don't have to keep getting up and down.
• Dessert and coffee can also be set on a tea cart or another small table. It obviates the necessity of clearing the big table while the guests are still there.
• You want to avoid traffic jams, so setting up what goes on the buffet table is an exercise in logic and function. I lay out my serving dishes the night before, with labels of what goes where set in front.
• When considering the color of your centerpiece, remember that food is color, and it will be on display with the china and tablecloth you've chosen.
• You should be able to eat any food served with a fork or spoon. It is difficult to use a knife while balancing a plate on your lap.
• Use large plates and oversized napkins.
• Have lots of small tables and chairs to encourage guests to sit comfortably.
• Use hot plates to keep the food on the buffet table warm.

🦋 ABOVE: A buffet line should flow smoothly so guests can proceed without backtracking. Plan ahead and place empty plates first and napkins and cutlery at either end. Then arrange the food in order of sequence, with the sauce directly next to the dish it complements. Use big rhubarb leaves if your table is large enough.

🦋 BELOW, FAR LEFT AND RIGHT: I prefer to use trays for buffets, especially when I serve desserts. Here, my collection of antique lace batiste mats and napkins are put to good use dressing up basic bamboo trays. Spoons and forks are wrapped in hosta leaves tied with lace.

🦋 BELOW LEFT: The busiest place is always where the drinks are served, so if you have sufficient space, arrange beverages on a separate table. I made these ice buckets using fresh petals and ferns.

🦋 BELOW RIGHT: Many people prefer to serve after-dinner coffee on a table or rolling trolley in the library or living room. There, guests can linger in front of a fireplace or just relax in an easy chair.

Chapter
6

🦋 LEFT: Southern
hospitality under the
graceful cover of an
elegant gazebo provides
a cool oasis featuring
oak-leaf and snowflake
hydrangea in bloom.
Areas like this in a
garden offer tranquil
places to relax and
entertain guests.
FOLLOWING PAGE: This
green and white table
setting reflects the
dappled tones in the
landscape. A dramatic
bouquet of Stargazer
lilies, rhododendron,
hydrangea, viburnum,
itea, parsley, and galax
flowers is at center.
DETAIL: An old market
basket contains
delicious breads and
cakes freshly baked for
a summer picnic.

Setting Tables Outside

porches • pools • gardens • gazebos

I always enjoyed Dorothy Frances Gurney's sweet poem "The kiss of the sun for pardon, the song of the birds for mirth; One is nearer God's heart in a garden than anywhere else on earth." Just being outside is heavenly, but eating outdoors is an even more sublime experience. It is one that we savor, especially when we're traveling in Italy. Food seems to taste better in the fresh air, whether it's an impromptu side-of-the-road picnic, a feast in a Tuscan garden, or a simple meal on a trattoria's terrace.

At home, we virtually live outside from the end of May to late autumn. The herb garden and terrace, grape arbor and porch are our favorite places to congregate with family and friends—everyone in a good mood, relaxing, chatting, and eating in the sun.

No matter where you choose to entertain outdoors—garden or yard, beach or pool side, boat deck, veranda, porch, or gazebo—the choice of menu and type of decoration will be determined by the location.

Entertaining outside has several advantages. You can more easily accommodate a large group of people, including energetic children. Nature is your

dining room so decorations can be inviting and inventive, using colors that don't have to match anything but your mood. Food can be light and seasonal and the atmosphere more informal.

Flowers should be abundant and natural. Stiff arrangements look out of place outside. Even if the occasion is more formal—an outdoor wedding, for example—flowers should still be loose and flowing. I also like to use oversized bowls of fruit or vegetables and even plants like topiaries and scented herbs in weathered pots or baskets. Big bouquets from the garden—old-fashioned roses in June, for instance—or wildflowers gathered in the meadow always look gorgeous set about in big old pitchers and pottery crocks.

When entertaining at night, **lighting** should be considered. Candles protected from drafts in glass or tin are always a sparkling addition to the table, as are torches and citronella candles, which deter insects. Place them strategically since their scent can be noticed.

Candles should be used on the buffet, so people can clearly see what is being served. To light walkways and paths, set candles into containers made

for this specific purpose. Accent your already existing lighting by stringing tiny white lights on tree branches and around gateposts and trellises.

Little touches are important. Cluster pots of scented herbs like lavender, rosemary, and southernwood here and there to deter bugs. Place straw hats and parasols around for your guests to use. Big muslin umbrellas set over tables in sunny locations keep people and food cooler.

Several days before your party, go outside at the same time you will be serving your guests to assess the location and see how much sun or shade you will have to deal with. Then decide where everything will go and where people will sit. Review your menu and how the food will be served. Make a list of what you will need outside, or else you will be running in and out all the time. If the event is a large one, a caterer or party planner could be the answer.

Always have lots of cool things to drink and be sure to have more than enough ice on hand. Outdoors is the perfect place for serving icy summer drinks like sangria, granitas, lemonade, and my favorite hot weather drink, iced tea. Here is my recipe, which makes twelve glasses:

Top Left: A screened porch is the perfect spot for a languid lunch. The main course, a salad of mesclun and edible flowers, is the centerpiece in an evocative setting of wicker and lace.

Center: A bright accent, the sunflower historically symbolizes the sun itself. Here they are cut short and inserted into water-filled flower tubes made for this purpose.

Bottom: In Italy a centerpiece grouping of various fruits in large dishes or bowls is called a *trionfo*. Here this *triumph* is arranged with grapes and sunflowers for a summer porch lunch.

Opposite: A picket fence surrounds a Victorian porch where a romantic meal is set with white flowers—pansies, hostas, hydrangeas, and Queen Anne's lace—in silver vases. Mother-of-pearl serving pieces and lace lend a delicate touch.

No-Fail Iced Tea

12 bags of your favorite tea
1 cup sugar
Lemon verbena or mint leaves
2 lemons

1. Boil three quarts of water.
2. Add the twelve teabags and steep for ten minutes, then remove.
3. Combine cup of sugar and ½ cup of water at high heat, stirring constantly until dissolved.
4. Add sugar mixture to the tea along with several crushed lemon verbena or mint leaves and let stand for one hour.
5. Remove the leaves and refrigerate.
6. Add two thinly sliced lemons, ice, and serve.

Good friends, good food, good wine, good weather make a great picnic. A day of antiquing may end with an alfresco picnic on the big lawn at Tanglewood listening to wonderful music. Although I don't pack as much as Mrs. Beeton recommended—everything from a stick of horseradish to four teapots—I still like to load our picnic hamper with an abundance of summer treats and great desserts. I always include a jar filled with water and a small bouquet for the center of our blanket.

OPPOSITE: Having breakfast outside is always a treat, especially if you have the morning to yourself. Little muffins serve as the decoration on a table of neutrals and naturals, from the pressed paper doilies to the butter crock and even the dried fruit.
ABOVE RIGHT: Gardens are splendid places for outdoor meals. In the center of this table is a lavender topiary and, on either side, little English clay pots filled with individual herbs—rosemary, sage, and pineapple mint. Pale pink napkins, pillows, and dishes accent the greens of the herb garden.
RIGHT: A visit to this garden luncheon will not be soon forgotten, as each guest will be given a fragrant potted herb as a remembrance.

🦋 PREVIOUS PAGE, LEFT: Dining on a terrace with the gentle sound of lapping water is one of life's pleasures. Favorite things like china and silver are brought from inside. A lively arrangement, including parrot tulips, viburnum, ranunculus, and anemones, is still no match for the stunning view.

🦋 PREVIOUS PAGE, RIGHT: A wonderful place to entertain in summer, this delightful pool house even has a fireplace for cooler days. The table is set with great personal style. The textures of the Adirondack tabletop, oversized mushroom, and various herbs work effortlessly with refined silver and linens.

🦋 OPPOSITE: A serene moment before guests arrive for a poolside buffet. Simple summer flowers and vegetables embellish the colorful table decorated with the hostess's airplane collection.

🦋 ABOVE, LEFT AND RIGHT: Queen Victoria said that "things taste better in small houses." The young mistress of this playhouse would agree. A tea party for teddy bears and a best friend is an excuse to use her grandma's Swedish china and flowers from her mother's garden, decorating little tables inside and out.

🦋 BELOW, LEFT AND RIGHT: A tailgate picnic is an opportunity to use all my tartan plaid accessories—blankets, picnic hampers, and napkins. I always pack a mason jar filled with water in which a wildflower bouquet will be placed. I also try not to forget to pack binoculars and my bird books.

Chapter 7

🦋 LEFT: Having people for tea is a perfect time to start decorating with edible flowers. This simple bundt cake is a family recipe. Butter cream frosting makes a neutral background for the blazing pansies in all their spring glory.
FOLLOWING PAGE: A tea table is accented with beautiful flowers, including tulips, roses, and delphinium. Stacks of tasty tea sandwiches embellished with vegetables and flowers are offered along with warm scones and Devonshire cream with strawberries.
DETAIL: A graceful Victorian silver ladle is filled with perky, colorful pansies.

Using Flowers in Food

easy recipes · edible accents

Frank Lloyd Wright once said, "Dining is and always was a great artistic opportunity." It certainly can be, especially if you go one step farther and decorate your food with flowers, leaves, and herbs, thus making the entire experience so much more beautiful and enticing. In addition, each small edible blossom is filled with flavor, a pleasure that in the past has often been underrated!

Edible flowers can transform the presentation of your food with colors that are vivid and varied. This is especially true if you are doing a buffet, tea party, or cocktail party where all the dishes are set out on the table at once, offering a visual feast as well as an edible one. Here are some of the many ways that flowers can be used creatively:

- Decorating the tops of cakes with blossoms can be attractive, particularly for special occasions like weddings, birthdays, and teas. Use brightly colored pansies, blue borage flowers with vivid orange zest, or else try flowers in monochromatic tones, such as pale blush to bright pink roses. Coordinate the flowers with the color scheme of the table, room, or theme of the event, and these cakes will end up being much more than just dessert.

- When choosing edible flowers for vegetable or fruit salads, use a vivid color scheme so the final result can serve as a stunning centerpiece. Eye-catching combinations can be made by combining fuschia rose petals, borage, chive blossoms and violets, or orange marigolds and nasturtiums.

- Try freezing small blossoms or herbs in ice cubes trays or decorative ice molds; floating them in beverages makes for a lovely little surprise. Tiny rose heads or violets in ice cubes can be added to drinks like plain water or iced tea. Mint or lemon balm leaves in cubes are the perfect complement to lemonade. Large ice molds dappled with flowers look elegant in silver or glass punch bowls filled to the brim with cold champagne or fruit punches.

- Using flowers to embellish the tops of pâtés, wheels of cheese, or any food with a flat top can be fun. You can make designs using leaves and whole sprigs of herbs. Fruits cut into shapes and whole flower heads also look appetizing.

- Frost flowers, small berries, and fruits with sugar to give a shimmering look to

compotes, cakes, and desserts like ice cream and sorbet. It's an easy task requiring only egg whites and sugar, and the simple directions for doing this are on page 52.

- Float color-coordinated blossoms like nasturtiums atop creamy soups like lobster bisque or cream of tomato. Other hot beverages such as tea can be made special with the addition of a violet blossom, or sprigs of an herb, like mint or lemon verbena.

- Creating attractive gifts for the kitchen can also be fun and economical. Edible blossoms and herbs can be made into delicious jams, jellies, vinegars, infused oils, and teas.

Before using any flower, you must first carefully identify them as edible, pesticide-free, and not poisonous or liable to cause an allergic reaction. Then sample them to be sure you find them palatable. Most taste the way they smell.

Buy edible flowers on the day you'll be using them, or gather them from the garden early that morning. Wash them thoroughly, then gently blot dry. Store everything, flower heads and petals, in a plastic bag in the refrigerator until you are ready to use them.

Following are two basic recipes of mine, plus a listing of edible flowers.

OPPOSITE: At this summer party in Birmingham, Alabama, caterer Kathy Mezrano uses edible flowers to make the food look even more beautiful. Pâté is embellished with chive blossoms and stalks, a sculptured red cabbage is filled with tortellini, and a floral ice mold floats atop champagne punch. Finger food like the stuffed endives also includes flowers.

ABOVE RIGHT: French Brie is covered with a pinwheel design of kiwi, strawberries, and melon. The individual cheesecakes are topped with snapdragons, sweet William blooms, and rose petals.

RIGHT: Lush pink roses are everywhere on this table, including in the ice cubes floating in the glass goblet.

Edible Flowers

- *Anise Hyssop*—Use the purple-colored flowers and leaves as a garnish, in teas, and in baking for a licorice flavor.
- *Borage*—Use the whole blue flower, which tastes a little like cucumber, in fruit cups, salads, or frozen into ice cubes.
- *Chives*—The mauve blossoms have a subtle onion flavor and are tasty on egg dishes and salads.
- *Lavender*—The bright purple flowers have a lemony taste and can be used for teas and to subtly scent sugar and honey.
- *Marigolds*—Use the bright orange petals for a saffron flavor in vegetables, poultry, eggs, rice, and salads.
- *Nasturtiums*—Use the whole yellowy orange blossoms and green leaves for a peppery flavor in soups and salads.
- *Pansies*—These are slightly spicy and especially nice for decorating cakes and on desserts like ice cream or sorbet.
- *Roses*—Use the petals for a subtle floral flavor in desserts and in drinks like iced tea, champagne, and rose hip tea.

Two-Step Salad Dressing

This recipe makes about 1 cup and is tasty on mixed green and edible flower salads.

> 2 tbs. red wine vinegar
> 1 tbs. balsamic vinegar
> 1 tsp. Dijon mustard
> 1 tsp. lemon juice
> $1/2$ tsp. sugar
> $1/4$ tsp. pepper and salt
> $1/2$ cup olive oil

1. Mix all ingredients except olive oil in a bowl. Then add the oil and whisk.
2. Pour over assorted greens and flowers. Toss to coat.

Making a Perfect Cup of Tea

Much is made of preparing tea properly, but my theory is, if you can boil water, you can make tea.

1. Fill a kettle with fresh cold water. Bring it to a full boil, then turn off immediately.
2. To prewarm the teapot, pour in a small amount of the hot water, swirling it about. Then discard.
3. Add the tea leaves to the pot, one spoon per cup, plus one for the pot, and then fill with the hot water. Stir to circulate.
4. Put lid back and, depending on the size of the leaves, let stand for 3 to 7 minutes for the tea to release its flavor. Then pour through a tea strainer into cups.
5. You can use this method to make floral and herbal teas, substituting flowers like anise hyssop, nasturtiums, rose petals, or violets for the tea leaves.

🦋 ABOVE: A tea tray is set with pink luster teacups and an unusual porcelain cookie jar, circa 1800.
LEFT: A turquoise plate frames a mesclun salad topped with vivid nasturtiums.
OPPOSITE: Edible flowers are particularly appropriate on cakes like this opulent wedding cake.

Chapter
8

LEFT: One of my favorite Christmas themes is using tartan plaids. The tablecloth is an antique Scottish shawl on which red-glass dishes and goblets sparkle. Little details like old postcards, place cards, tree napkin rings, plaid ribbons, and a tartan fabric ornament, which can be taken home by guests as a token, all enliven the table.
FOLLOWING PAGE: Christmas means adding small touches all around the house, like this sweet silver cup engraved with the words "Imogene's first Christmas, from Grandma."
DETAIL: A welcoming wreath of cranberries and magnolia leaves.

Celebrating Christmas

setting • wrapping • trimming

"So now is come our joyfulest feast; Let every man be jolly. Each room with ivy leaves is dressed, and every post with holly." These words, written over a hundred years ago, illustrate that, happily, not much has changed about Christmas. December is a magical month, a time of goodwill and family gatherings. And though its real significance is religious, most of us look at Christmas through the eyes of children—Santa Claus, mistletoe, gifts, overflowing stockings, turkey, carol singing, and, of course, the Christmas tree.

When I was a child, our tree was hung with the same treasured ornaments that we carefully unpacked from their nest of yellowing newspapers each year, reading the old ads as we decorated the tree. I still have my favorite ornament, an iridescent glass swan. Each time I look at it, I reflect on past holidays and realize that for me—and, indeed, for most of us— Christmas means tradition and heartfelt associations. How we decorate our homes and tables at this time of year reflects those particular memories.

I always start with the front door. I agree with the old saying: "A threshold is a sacred thing." Wreaths or door bouquets always welcome guests. At this time of year there are all kinds of greens available, including hemlock, pine, western cedar, juniper, mistletoe, holly, spruce, fir, ivy, pittosporum, and boxwood, to name a few. Use what nature has to offer to decorate not only the front door but mantelpieces, banisters, sideboards, and the table.

The aromas of Christmas also help set the mood. Herbs and spices like cinnamon sticks, whole cloves, and bay leaf added to a pot of simmering water will scent the rooms with a spicy fragrance. I fill bowls throughout the house with Cherchez's Sixteenth-Century Rondelitia potpourri, which was a favorite royal blend of spices with lavender. Christmas trees also impart their own fresh fragrance. And I often use a live miniature tree, wrapped in silk tartan plaid ribbons, as a centerpiece. In fact, last year our Christmas tree was a live one that was then planted outside to be enjoyed forever. If you are considering using live trees as decorations, the following tips should be helpful:

- Buy a tree labeled "root pruned" at a reputable nursery and choose a type that will do well in your area.
- Remember to dig a hole in early fall

Easy Christmas Ideas

Make every corner of your home beautiful with these simple ideas that say "Merry Christmas."

before the ground freezes and cover it with straw or plastic to prevent freezing. Store the soil you have dug out in a warm place, like a heated garage so you can use it to plant the tree easily after Christmas.

- The height of the tree determines the size and weight of the root ball, so keep your choice manageable.
- Put the tree in a cool place for two days to adjust before planting it outside, in a garage or potting shed, for example.
- Remember to water your tree when it is in the house *and* when planted outside.

TOP LEFT: Create a fantasy by hanging Christmas ornaments from chandeliers over tables and in living areas. Choose designs that coordinate, like these shimmering hand-blown glass grapes in brilliant colors.

TOP RIGHT: Kissing balls, a Victorian tradition, are hung over doorways or from a chandelier. This one was made by gluing sheet moss and a garland of fake fruit over a Styrofoam ball with a hot glue gun.

MIDDLE LEFT: Make centerpieces from things you already have. This one consists of an antique wooden sled filled with princess pine and assorted handmade ornaments given to me by many friends over the years.

MIDDLE RIGHT: Each corner of the room should be festive. Fill compotes like this old French milk-glass bowl with red fruits like lady apples, cranberries, or cherries and tie with a gossamer ribbon.

BOTTOM LEFT: The delicious scents of Christmas that waft through your home could include fresh-baked gingerbread, balsam holiday greens, and fragrant spicy potpourri set in big bowls on side tables.

BOTTOM RIGHT: Friends always leave our house with a little something at this time of the year. I like to tie hand-sewn stockings to each dining chair and fill them with homemade goodies.

RIGHT: If you have as many extra Christmas tree ornaments as we do, they can be put to good use by tying them around napkins with festive ribbons and a sprig of green, as we have here.

If you prefer a cut tree, you will be able to trim some fragrant boughs off for other uses, especially centerpieces. When purchasing it, bounce the tree on the stump end to make sure the needles are flexible and don't fall off. Buy your tree at a reputable nursery and choose a type that will do well in your area. If you live in the Northeast or Northcentral United States, look for Fraser or Scotch pine; in the Northwest, Noble or Douglas fir; in the South, Leland cypress or holly; in the Southwest, Monterey pine or Arizona cypress. To prolong the life of the tree, place it in a cool part of the room and water it frequently.

Trimming our Christmas tree is a trip down memory lane. It is hung with decorations from family and friends, and treasures handmade by the children. We no longer exchange gifts with our closest friends, preferring to donate what we would have spent on each other to a different charity each year. Instead, we exchange small tree ornaments. Our collection has now grown from the ridiculous to the sublime. As a result, I've had to think of new ways to use them.

Ornaments dress up the table in many ways. Sometimes I'll fill a big basket or an old miniature sled with orna-

🕊 OPPOSITE: This dazzling table set for Christmas awaits the arrival of family and friends. Golden touches weave their magic from the thick cords on the garland-draped banister to the table cover of net stars, the classic pedestals holding grape topiaries, passementerie napkin ties, lace paper doilies, and sparkling wine.

ABOVE RIGHT: Brass candlesticks light the way, each opulently decorated with a bobèche, a gold wreath, and a sprig of boxwood. The hand-painted nineteenth-century sprig china dinner service has many serving pieces.

RIGHT: These wooden architectural Christmas tree ornaments are from a collection that a friend has handcrafted for her charming shop. At holiday time, they decorate her tree and table as well. I also like to tie them onto Christmas gift boxes.

🦋 Above: It's Christmas morning. Little voices fill the house and the table is set for a holiday breakfast. The centerpiece is a spun-wire tree hung with antique children's toys and treasures of Christmases past.
Opposite: Tabletops twinkle with gold and silver. Big gold pinecones cluster under a glass pedestal that holds shiny pears, apples, and artichokes. Gold papers and ribbons can be found at craft stores, which are filled with ideas at holiday time. Tie ornaments onto decanters and put favors at each place.

ments and use it as a centerpiece. They also look festive tied onto napkin rings or onto the backs of dining chairs. Tie coordinating ornaments onto your chandelier with pretty ribbons.

Twinkling candles capture the Christmas spirit wherever they are placed, so use them liberally. This is the time to bring out your grandmother's ornate silver candelabra or those votives for each place setting. Decorate candlesticks imaginatively, using everything from cinnamon sticks (see p. 107) to candle rings and ribbons.

Gold, silver, and white all gleam on the table at holiday time. Spray-paint pinecones, leaves, acorns, nuts, and other dried material for use in your centerpieces. Use gold or silver lamé as a table covering as did the famous decorator Elsie De Wolfe. Visit your local craft stores, which can be a great source of creative and inexpensive ideas.

Consider using all red or white flowers: poinsettias, roses, orchids, carnations, tulips, freesias, potted paper whites, and amaryllis. Place cards, Christmas crackers, favors, silver dishes filled with candies—these details all add to the pleasures of a congenial holiday table.

Put the focus back on the *spirit* of the holidays. Christmas is all about children—not just about the gifts they receive, but about what they share. Children love to help and seem to have more patience for making things when there is a goal in mind. Involve them in every aspect of holiday making, creating easy things like gift tags, dried fruit garlands, edible ornaments for the birds, sachets, cookies, topiaries, and little pomanders made of lady apples and lemons. I have a bowl of misshapen pomanders that I wouldn't trade for a million dollars that my nieces and nephews made for Christmas fifteen years ago.

Get your children to help wrap gifts in all types of recycled paper. Newspapers, old maps, and Kraft paper all look beautiful tied with elegant ribbons that can themselves be recycled.

🦋 ABOVE LEFT: Place cards are a good idea at holidays, when there are so many people and seating can be confusing. Make these by writing with a gold or silver felt-tipped pen on any flat leaf, like the magnolia shown here, or ivy, holly, galax, or rhododendron. Press the leaf under a heavy book for several hours. Lean leaves up against glasses, tuck them into napkins or place in the center of a plate.

ABOVE RIGHT: Children love to help make Christmas crackers, which are simple to make and fun to fill.

Fill a big basket on the hall table with batches of Christmas cookies and sugar plums wrapped in colored cellophane and gay ribbons. Send your guests off with a little token from you and your family. Your children can help you make these using the recipe from my little book *Merry Christmas.* Remember John Greenleaf Whittier's wonderful thought, "For somehow, not only at Christmas, but all the year through, the joy that you give to others is the joy that comes back to you."

One of the nicest holiday traditions to come to us from Britain is Christmas crackers, which are placed at each holiday table setting. When you and your neighbor each pull an end, it pops, revealing party favors like miniature objects, toys, and candy. With the following directions, you can make your own. They won't pop like the ones you buy, but you can create special ones by filling them with miniature theme tokens like golf or gardening ornaments, gift certificates, coins, even jewelry. Use beautiful wrapping papers or colorful amusing ones for children.

Christmas Crackers

Cardboard tube
Wrapping paper
Rubber cement or glue
Rubber band
1 yard of ¹/₂-inch ribbon

1. Using a knife, carefully cut off a 5-inch section from an empty paper towel roll. Slit it lengthwise down the center and press open with your hand, flattening it a bit.

2. Cut a piece of wrapping paper 15 inches long and 8 inches wide.

3. Place the cardboard tube in the center of the paper, slit side up. Glue the tube to the wrapping paper using rubber cement or paper glue.

4. When dry, fill the tube with the gifts. Roll one side of the wrapping paper to overlap the other. Glue down and hold together with a rubber band.

5. Gather the paper tightly and tie at each end with a pretty coordinating ribbon about 18 inches long. Remove rubber band from the center.

🦋 ABOVE LEFT: Wrapping a pillar candle with cinnamon sticks turns a simple candle into something special.
RIGHT: Another way to decorate candles is to make a cranberry star and tie it on with satin ribbon.

Decorating Holiday Candles

Candlelight on the table at holiday time creates a festive mood. Pour off accumulated wax as the evening progresses and never leave candles unattended.

Cinnamon Stick Wrap

*3-inch cinnamon sticks
(for around your candle)
2-inch pillar candle
Rubber band
Wired ribbon or natural raffia*

1. Stand the cinnamon sticks next to one another halfway around the candle and rubber band them tightly into place.
2. Add the remaining cinnamon sticks, covering the rest of the candle.
3. Tightly tie wired ribbon or raffia around the middle and bow.

Cranberry Star

*Bag of dried cranberries
12 inches of florist wire
18 inches of satin ribbon*

1. Thread the cranberries onto the wire through their center, leaving 1 inch of wire at each end.
2. Twist both ends together securely, making a loop with the wire.
3. Sharply indent the wire 5 times to make a star pattern.
4. Tie a ribbon through the loop and onto a candlestick.

🦋 BELOW, LEFT AND RIGHT: All you'll need for decorating your candles festively at holiday time.

Chapter 9

LEFT: Bringing
the outside inside is
what this cute Easter
setting is all about.
Real grass was used to
cover the entire table.
FAR LEFT: In nineteenth-
century Russia, Fabergé
eggs were tucked into
napkins as favors. Alas,
ours are not Fabergé.
FOLLOWING PAGE: Whether
at a big party or a more
intimate gathering, it's
always nice to mark the
arrival of the New Year
with a celebration. A
shimmering table set
with gold and silver is
topped with a mobile
of glittering stars.
DETAIL: When I'm not
using this old ice bucket
to chill champagne,
I use it for flowers.

Special Occasions

holidays • parties • birthdays

Shakespeare said, "Small cheer and great welcome makes a merry feast!" Special occasions in our lives should indeed be celebrated with joy, enlivened by good friends and family, beautiful flowers and decorations, and delicious food. Birthdays, baby showers, christenings, bar mitzvahs, weddings, anniversaries, New Year's, Valentine's Day, Easter, July Fourth, Thanksgiving, and Christmas are all occasions when we can pull out the stops and be as extravagantly creative as we want.

The prospect of New Year's Eve, not everyone's favorite evening, can be daunting. It's a perfect time to invite good friends over for an easy evening—especially the friends who fear staying home almost more than going out.

I edit down after Christmas, but continue spray-painting—silver instead of gold—to transform dried botanicals like poppy pods, pinecones, pomegranates, and artichokes. Silver wrapping paper and aluminum foil get wrapped around flowerpots and other containers and then tied with silver tassels.

Serving champagne or champagne punch makes the occasion extra special. After all, Dom Perignon, the blind monk who discovered champagne, exclaimed, when he first sipped it, "Come quickly, I am tasting the stars." Only wines made in the Champagne region of France can be called Champagne with a capital "C." The others must be labeled with a lowercase "c." If you open the bottle correctly, there won't be the sound of an explosion, but only a slight pop.

If you are having a large group of people over, you might want to make champagne punch. This easy recipe, which serves about sixteen people, is lovely looking as well as luscious. Wrap little golden wire stars around the stems of the champagne flutes.

Champagne Punch

2 cups cranberry juice
4 cups orange juice
1/4 cup lemon juice
4 cups seltzer
1 bottle champagne
2 cups superfine sugar
1 cup water
6 ounces frozen lemonade
  concentrate
1 pint strawberries

1. The day before, chill the juices, the seltzer, and the champagne.

2. Then, in a saucepan, bring the sugar, water, and lemonade concentrate to a boil until dissolved. Pour into a container and refrigerate.

3. To make the punch, hull the strawberries, puree them in a blender, and then strain them into a punch bowl. Stir in the sugar mixture, juices, seltzer, and champagne. Add ice and serve.

I like to help speed up the arrival of spring by making a big fuss about Easter as the Easter bunny is considered a very special guest in our house! Tables can be colorfully decorated. A friend uses fresh sod as a tablecloth—the Russian Romanoffs celebrated with priceless Fabergé eggs. Either way, there is an endless choice of possibilities. Start with thatchy baskets, tied with ribbons in vivid colors, and fill them with goodies. Make smaller ones for each place setting. Line the big ones with green moss to make centerpieces filled with the first potted primroses of spring.

Memorial Day, Labor Day, and July Fourth are when the spirit of America is commemorated. We use a red, white, and blue theme, with a big flag hanging from the porch, bunting everywhere, miniature flags set into centerpieces of seasonal

TOP LEFT: The glory of autumn colors gives this tabletop a special liveliness at Thanksgiving, with the combination of pumpkins, gourds, Chinese lanterns, apples, and multicolored vines.

CENTER: Certain fruits and vegetables like artichokes, gourds, and apples make unusual candleholders when the center is hollowed out.

BOTTOM: To spread the holiday spirit around the house, fill bowls with arrangements of small citrus fruits or scented potpourri. Dried pieces of orange peel studded with cloves smell lovely.

OPPOSITE: Tableware complements the season, with twig mats and cutlery, embossed place cards, silk maple leaves tucked into napkin rings, and coordinated china and glasses.

vegetables, and pies and cakes decorated with blueberries and strawberries.

Thanksgiving ushers in a season with the bursting rich colors of autumn—oranges, browns, golds. It's a time for families to celebrate the bounty and peace that we sometimes take for granted. Take long walks and gather materials for decorating—bittersweet, rose hips, dried grasses, and branches with colorful leaves, as well as berries and seed heads.

Buy abundant seasonal offerings at your local market like Chinese lanterns, eucalyptus, pomegranates, pumpkins, fall squash and gourds in myriad shapes and textures, apples, pears, and nuts. Hollow out pumpkins and melons to use as containers for your arrangements or apples and gourds to hold candles.

Other occasions—like weddings, anniversaries, and birthdays—are perfect opportunities to have parties. Depending on the number of people you intend to invite, this is the moment to consider whether you need caterers, party planners, floral designers, and companies that specialize in all the facets of party-giving, from tents to tableware. How many people are coming? Will the party be at home, in a hotel, club, restaurant, or in a garden? Is the event formal or informal? All these questions will have to be answered before you get started.

OPPOSITE: This very lucky sixteen-year-old has a wonderful godmother who loves to entertain. The table awaits the arrival of sixteen friends who will celebrate her birthday in an elegant setting of antique Swiss-glass vases filled with delicate old-fashioned nosegays. Gossamer ribbons are tied on the thoughtful favors at each place setting.

ABOVE RIGHT: This dining room is the perfect place to have a splendid party. The mirrors provide a luminous background for the candlelit Oriental theme. Pottery chargers act as mats for the folded napkins holding silver chopsticks.

RIGHT: A masterpiece of Zen-like simplicity: individual flowers and leaves in a silver tray.

Parties for children, especially birthdays, should be fun. These adorable girls celebrate in the Southern tradition with lots of lacy frills, which appear on the beaded doilies, atop the frosty drinks, in the creamy butter icing on the flower-bedecked cake, and even on their frothy handmade Victorian-style batiste dresses.

🦋 ABOVE: An old candle-ring surrounds the cake and mirrors are decorated with each child's name.

Develop a theme for your party, and coordinate the flowers with table linens, even tent linings and chair coverings. Decide on what flowers you want to use—they can be a very effective theme on their own. Remember that your centerpieces will be duplicated on each table, so they should be smashing.

Planning parties yourself, especially for those you love, can be a wonderful experience. A cake decorated with flowers or miniature toys can be the centerpiece at a child's birthday party; place a teapot with flowers at the center of a luncheon table for the surprise party of a friend; use enlarged old photos in the centerpiece of an anniversary celebration for parents—all ensure that a special occasion will be a shared remembrance for years to come.

🦋 BELOW: The chairs are adorned with little rose-filled antique baskets, tied on with ribbons.

🦋 LEFT: A montage of photographs taken during my travels, including signs from roadside stands, nurseries, local farmers' markets, gardens, and a tearoom at Christine's, one of my favorite shops in the South. FOLLOWING PAGE: The lavender patch that sits outside our vegetable garden is a source of great satisfaction. The hidcote lavender bushes, planted many years ago, produce a bountiful and fragrant harvest each summer. DETAIL: From a collection of old watering cans, this one is used for flower arrangements as well as its original purpose.

Finding Inspiration

here • there • everywhere

"Flowers always make people better, happier, and more helpful; they are sunshine, food, and medicine to the soul." I'm inspired by flowers wherever I go and read these words of Luther Burbank on a trip to the Napa Valley in California, which included a visit to his birthplace, Santa Rosa.

I like visiting new places because I am constantly foraging about for creative stimulus. Sometimes this is nothing more than flipping through a magazine, or discovering a pretty new place for lunch. But a big trip or vacation always clears the mind and opens the eyes to seeing ordinary things in a new way.

My tabletops look the way they do as a result of my peregrinations. I'm writing this on the way home from spending a week in Maine, where we took lots of long walks on the beach. The seashells I've collected will be well used. People are always asking me where they can get ideas for decorating the table, so I'll share some suggestions with you here.

I suggest visiting your local markets—there are surprises there. I try to cook and decorate the table in rhythm with the seasons, so a stop at the **farmers' market** in our little town often results in new unanticipated ideas for centerpieces—a big basket of eggplants in different shades of lavender or putting many varieties of autumn squash in a shiny green bowl, for instance.

When traveling, I make a beeline to these lively local places and get great ideas I can try at home. France and Italy are filled with markets that contain the freshest of everything grown in the surrounding countryside. Some of my favorites in Italy are the Rialto in Venice, and the Mercato Centrale in Florence. I love the little ones in almost every town in France, especially the year-round market in Aix-en-Provence, and Rungis outside of Paris. Closer to home, the Union Square Greenmarket at East 17th Street and Broadway in New York City continues to expand each year, carrying everything from fresh-baked doughnuts to gorgeous flowers, all locally produced.

Nurseries and farm stands are good places to buy botanicals. Potted plants and seasonal offerings like dried flowers and holiday wreaths can usually be had at reasonable prices. And you will be supporting local small businesses with your purchases, which is something we should all make an attempt to do.

🕊 ABOVE LEFT: Tall foxgloves growing at Old Westbury Gardens, Long Island. RIGHT: Summer flowers on our favorite table at the Locanda Cipriani. OPPOSITE: The beautiful herb garden at the Hotel Bel-Air in California.

You might wonder why anyone would go to a **florist** when flowers are now readily available in so many different locations. Two good reasons are taste and quality. Florists generally stock the best-quality flowers obtainable, and they condition them properly so they will last once you get them home.

If you use the same florist regularly, he or she will be more inclined to order special things for you. If your tastes are similar, you'll find that you can trust the florist to come up with something special. I am also particular when I send flowers to someone. With a good florist, you can feel confident that a gift of flowers ordered over the phone will be put together with taste.

Whenever I'm ordering flowers outside my florist's delivery area, I specify a particular color palette—like a range of pinks, blues, or all whites—and mention some favorite flowers in these colors that I would like included. This way, I know my taste level will be maintained.

Visiting a **flower show** can be an unforgettable experience. There are a number of excellent flower shows that I enjoy and come away from with lots of ideas as well as seeds and seedlings.

When I'm in London, I try not to miss the Chelsea Flower Show. It's an extraordinary event, and tickets are always at a premium. However, if you join the Royal Horticultural Society, you may buy your

🕊 Tabletop ideas are everywhere. BELOW LEFT: The Dining Trade, and MIDDLE: Williams-Sonoma, both in New York City. RIGHT: Silamar Farm in Millerton, New York. OPPOSITE: Homewood House in Baltimore.

🦋 OPPOSITE TOP: Colorful berries on display at the Rialto Market in Venice. ABOVE LEFT: Breads at the farmers' market in Millbrook. MIDDLE: A favorite plate. RIGHT: Wire jardinieres and plants for future tabletops.

tickets in advance. I've included a list of these shows in the Source Guide.

Historic homes and gardens are an enormous source of ideas and repositories of elegance and style. There you can study museum-quality tableware and get great setting ideas too. A visit to a garden designed by a respected landscape architect is an opportunity to be introduced to new botanicals to use in your own arrangements and gardens.

If you're having a meal in a fine **restaurant,** note how they have decorated the table. One of our favorites, the Locanda Cipriani on Torcello near Venice, where the flower-laden tables sit surrounded by gardens and grape arbors, inspires even the most jaded eye.

Tabletop stores are a source of terrific ideas. Their job is to cover the various markets in depth and choose the best. Antiques shows and stores are also a good source for items that bring grace to any table. I love strolling through these antiques emporiums, where I'm reminded of how little has changed.

Though things do go in and out of fashion, the fact still remains that hospitality depends as much on welcoming surroundings, enthusiastic conversation, and nurturing thoughts as it does on good food and beautiful tables. We must keep in mind Ralph Waldo Emerson's excellent advice, "The ornament of a house is the friends that frequent it!"

🦋 OPPOSITE BOTTOM: Windowsill decorations will be used later, clustered on the dining table. BELOW LEFT: Our cutting garden in June, with roses and poppies in bloom. RIGHT: A lovely thought on a vintage sampler.

Yours is the earth and Everything in it

Source Guide

"You will find out that there are all sorts of ways of learning, not only from people and books, but from sheer trying."

—GERTRUDE JEYKLL

These shops, some of my favorites, carry wonderful linens, glass, china, flatware, or a combination of these items. Those with primarily antique tableware are noted.

Alabama

Bromberg & Company
2800 Cahaba Rd.
Mountain Brook, AL 35223
(205) 871-3276

Christine's
2822 Petticoat Lane
Mountain Brook, AL 35223
(205) 871-8297

Interior's Market
2812 Second Ave. S.
Birmingham, AL 35223
(205) 323-2817
Antique china, silver, glass

Past Pleasures Antiques
314 Magnolia Ave.
Fairhope, AL 36532
(334) 928-8484
Antique silver search

Queenie's Limited
1511 Ridge Rd.
Birmingham, AL 35223
(205) 870-0209
By appointment

Table Matters
2409 Montevallo Rd.
Birmingham, AL 35223
(205) 879-2730

California

Gumps
135 Post St.
San Francisco, CA 94108
1-800-766-7628
Catalog by mail
1-800-284-8677

Pottery Barn
For store nearest you:
1-800-922-5507

Vanderbilt & Company
1429 Main St.
St. Helena, CA 94574
(703) 963-1010

Williams-Sonoma
For store nearest you:
1-800-541-2233

Illinois

Crate & Barrel
For store nearest you:
1-800-323-5461

Massachusetts

The Coffman's Antiques Market
Jenifer House Commons
Route 7
Great Barrington, MA 01230
(413) 528-9282

The Country Dining Room Antiques
178 Main St.
Great Barrington, MA 01230
(413) 528-5050
Antique china, silver, glass

Olde Antiques Market
Jenifer House Commons
Route 7
Great Barrington, MA 01230
(413) 528-1840

Shreve, Crump & Low
330 Boylston St.
Boston, MA 02116
1-800-225-7088

New York

ABC Carpet & Home
888 Broadway
New York, NY 10003
(212) 473-3000

A.D.C. Heritage
485 Park Ave.
New York, NY 10022
(212) 750-2664
Antique silver

Ad Hoc Softwares
410 W. Broadway
New York, NY 10012
(212) 925-2652

A La Vieille Russie Antiques
781 Fifth Ave.
New York, NY 10022
(212) 752-1727
Antique silver, china, glass

Baccarat
625 Madison Ave.
New York, NY 10022
(212) 826-4100
1-800-777-0100

Bardith Ltd. Antiques
901 Madison Ave.
New York, NY 10021
(212) 737-3775
Antique china, glass

Barneys
660 Madison Ave.
New York, NY 10021
(212) 826-8900

Bergdorf Goodman
754 Fifth Ave.
New York, NY 10019
(212) 753-7300

E. Braun & Co.
717 Madison Ave.
New York, NY 10021
(212) 838-0650

Bridge Kitchenware
214 E. 52nd St.
New York, NY 10022
1-800-274-3435

Buccellati
46 E. 57th St.
New York, NY 10022
(212) 308-2900

Cartier
653 Fifth Ave.
New York, NY 10022
(212) 446-3460

Chez Grand'mere
24 Tinker St.
Woodstock, NY 12498
(914) 679-8140

Christofle
680 Madison Ave.
New York, NY 10021
(212) 308-9390

Coconut Co.
131 Greene St.
New York, NY 10012
(212) 539-1940

Daum Boutique
694 Madison Ave.
New York, NY 10021
(212) 355-2060

Dean & Deluca
560 Broadway
New York, NY 10012
(212) 431-1691

The Dining Table
306 E. 61st St.
New York, NY 10021
(212) 755-2304
By appointment

Felissimo
10 W. 56th St.
New York, NY 10019
(212) 956-4438
1-800-565-6785

Fortunoff
681 Fifth Ave.
New York, NY 10022
(212) 758-6660
Antique silver

Frette
799 Madison Ave.
New York, NY 10021
(212) 988-5221
1-800-355-Frette

Gucci
685 Fifth Ave.
New York, NY 10022
(212) 826-2600

Hoya Crystal Gallery
689 Madison Ave.
New York, NY 10021
(212) 223-6335

James II Galleries
15 E. 57th St.
New York, NY 10022
(212) 355-7040
Antique china, silver, glass

Georg Jensen
683 Madison Ave.
New York, NY 10021
(212) 759-6457

Kentshire Galleries, Ltd.
37 E. 12th St.
New York, NY 10003
(212) 673-6644
Antique china, silver, glass

Alice Kwartler Antiques
123 E. 57th St.
New York, NY 10022
(212) 752-3590
Antique silver

Lalique
680 Madison Ave.
New York, NY 10021
1-800-993-2580

Lamalle Kitchenware
36 W. 25th St.
New York, NY 10010
1-800-660-0750

Léron
750 Madison Ave.
New York, NY 10021
(212) 249-3188

MacKenzie-Childs
824 Madison Ave.
New York, NY 10021
(212) 570-6050

Frank McIntosh Home Collection
   at Henri Bendel
712 Fifth Ave.
New York, NY 10019
(212) 247-1100

Millbrook Antiques Center
Franklin Ave.
Millbrook, NY 12545
(914) 677-3921

Millbrook Antiques Mall
Franklin Ave.
Millbrook, NY 12545
(914) 677-9311

Moss
146 Greene St.
New York, NY 10012
(212) 226-2190

Simon Pearce
120 Wooster St.
New York, NY 10012
(212) 334-2393

Portico Home
379 West Broadway
New York, NY 10012
(212) 941-7800

Platypus
126 Spring St.
New York, NY 10012
(212) 219-3919

Polo-Ralph Lauren
650 Madison Ave.
New York, NY 10022
(212) 318-7000

Porthault
18 E. 69th St.
New York, NY 10021
(212) 688-1660

Portico Bed and Bath
139 Spring St.
New York, NY 10013
(212) 941-7722

Pratesi
829 Madison Ave.
New York, NY 10021
(212) 288-2315

James Robinson
480 Park Ave.
New York, NY 10022
(212) 752-6166
Antique china, silver, glass

Schweitzer Linen
1132 Madison Ave.
New York, NY 10028
1-800-554-6367

S.J. Shrubsole
104 E. 57th St.
New York, NY 10022
(212) 753-8920
Antique silver

Solanee
866 Lexington Ave.
New York, NY 10021
(212) 439-6109
1-800-71-Solan

Takashimaya
693 Fifth Ave.
New York, NY 10022
1-800-753-2038

Tiffany
Fifth Ave. at 57th St.
New York, NY 10022
(212) 755-8000

Tudor Rose Antiques
28 E. 10th St.
New York, NY 10003
(212) 677-5239
Antique silver

Village Antique Center
Franklin Ave.
Millbrook, NY 12545
(914) 677-5160

Waterford Wedgwood
713 Madison Ave.
New York, NY 10021
(212) 759-0500

Wolfman Gold and Good
    Company
116 Greene St.
New York, NY 10012
(212) 431-1888

S. Wyler Inc.
941 Lexington Ave.
New York, NY 10021
(212) 879-9848
Antique silver

Zona
97 Greene St.
New York, NY 10012
(212) 925-6750

Ohio

Flowers of the Meadow
7744 Laurel Ave.
Cincinnati, OH 45243
(513) 561-0882

Oregon

Bernadette Breu Antiques &
    Ornaments
241 S.W. Stark St.
Portland, OR 97204
(503) 294-1812
Antique china, silver, glass

Bloom's
449 Third St.
Lake Oswego, OR 97034
(503) 636-5876

Stars Antique Mall
7027 S.E. Milwaukie
Portland, OR 97204
(503) 239-0346

South Carolina

Geo. C. Birlant & Co.
191 King St.
Charleston, SC 29401
(803) 722-3842
Antique china, silver

Home
268 King St.
Charleston, SC 29401
(803) 723-9063

Christian Michi
220 King St.
Charleston, SC 29401
(803) 723-0575

152 A.D.
152 King St.
Charleston, SC 29401
(803) 577-7042
Antique china

Jack Patla Company
181 King St.
Charleston, SC 29401
(803) 723-2314
Antique china, silver

Texas

Lady Primrose's
500 Crescent Court
Dallas, TX 75201
(214) 871-8333
Antique china, silver, glass

Neiman Marcus
1618 Main St.
Dallas, TX 75201
1-800-825-8000

Florists

Here are some of my favorite places to buy cut flowers and flowers already arranged.

Blue Meadows Flowers
328 E. 11th St.
New York, NY 10003
(212) 979-8618

Christian Tortu at
  Takashimaya
693 Fifth Ave.
New York, NY 10022
(212) 350-0100

James Corcoran Flowers
1026 Lexington Ave.
New York, NY 10021
(212) 717-5780

J. Barry Ferguson
P.O. Box 176
Oyster Bay, NY 11771
(516) 922-0005

F.T.D. Florist
1-800-736-3333
For the florist nearest you

Larkspur
39 Eighth Ave.
New York, NY 10014
(212) 727-0587

David Madison Horticultural
  Design
219 E. 60th St.
New York, NY 10022
(212) 421-8110

Ronaldo Maia
27 E. 67th St.
New York, NY 10021
(212) 288-1049

Manhattan Fruitier
102 E. 29th St.
New York, NY 10016
(212) 686-0404

Marlo Flowers
428A E. 75th St.
New York, NY 10021
(212) 628-2246

Maxim's Flowers
680 Madison Ave.
New York, NY 10021
(212) 752-9889

1-800-Flowers
1600 Stewart Ave.
Westbury, NY 11590
1-800-Flowers

Oppizzi & Company, Ltd.
818 Greenwich St.
New York, NY 10014
(212) 633-2248

Perriwater Ltd.
960 First Ave.
New York, NY 10022
(212) 759-9313

Renny
505 Park Ave.
New York, NY 10022
(212) 288-7000

Salou
105 W. 72nd St.
New York, NY 10023
(212) 595-9604

Spring St. Gardens
186½ Spring St.
New York, NY 10012
(212) 966-2015

VSF
204 W. 10th St.
New York, NY 10014
(212) 206-7236

Zeze
398 E. 52nd St.
New York, NY 10022
(212) 753-7767

Wholesale Flower Markets

Bill's Flower Market
816 Sixth Ave.
New York, NY 10001
(212) 889-8154

Caribbean Cuts
120 W. 28th St.
New York, NY 10001
(212) 924-6969

Dutch Flower Line
148 W. 28th St.
New York, NY 10001
(212) 727-8600

Fischer & Page
134 W. 28th St.
New York, NY 10001
(212) 645-4106

Superior Florists
828 Sixth Ave.
New York, NY 10001
(212) 684-2595

York Floral Co.
104 W. 27th St.
New York, NY 10001
(212) 627-1840

Floral and Craft Supplies

Many of the things you need for flower arranging are available from the suppliers listed here.

Best Buy Floral Supply
P.O. Box 1982
Cedar Rapids, IA 52406
1-800-553-8497

Dorothy Biddle Service
HC 01 Box 900
Greeley, PA 18425
(717) 226-3239

Cindy's Garden
P.O. Box 50718
Pasadena, CA 91115
(818) 441-6564

Clapper's
1125 Washington St.
W. Newton, MA 02165
(617) 244-7909

Country Casual
17317 Germantown Rd.
Germantown, MD 20874
1-800-872-8325

Country House Floral Supply
P.O. Box 4086
BVL Station
Andover, MA 01810
(508) 475-8463

Frank's Nursery & Crafts
6501 E. Nevada
Detroit, MI 48234
(313) 366-8400
(Call for nearest store)

Gardener's Eden
P.O. Box 7307
San Francisco, CA 94120
(415) 421-4242

Gardener's Supply
128 Intervale Rd.
Burlington, VT 05401
(802) 863-1700

Smith & Hawken
25 Corte Madera
Mill Valley, CA 94941
(415) 383-2000

Where to Find

*This list includes places
where you can order many
of the items I used for the ideas
and projects in this book.*

Angelo Bonita
Floral Events Unlimited
2700 Garfield Ave.
Silver Springs, MD 20910
(301) 585-2772
Fresh nosegays and flowers

Central Shippee Inc.
46 Star Lake Rd.
Bloomingdale, NJ 07403
1-800-631-8968
Craft felt

Cherchez
P.O. Box 550
Millbrook, NY 12545
1-800-422-1744
Fragrance for the home

Cherishables
1608 20th St., N.W.
Washington, DC 20009
(202) 785-4087
Christmas ornaments

Floria
10500 Greenacres Dr.
Silver Springs, MD 20903
(301) 681-7157
Dried flower arrangements

Godiva Chocolatier
1-800-9-Godiva
Chocolates

Green Valley Growers
10450 Cherry Ridge Rd.
Sebastopol, CA 95472
(707) 823-5583
Fresh/dried hydrangeas

Kate's Paperie
8 W. 13th St.
New York, NY 10011
(212) 633-0570
Acid-free tissue paper

Now & Forever
Brambly Meadow
    Dorset, VT 05251
    (802) 867-4456
    Dried flower arrangements

Meadows Direct
13805 Highway 136
Onslow, IO 53231
(319) 485-2723
1-800-542-9771
Dried botanicals

Minka
4 Via Parigi
Palm Beach, FL 33480
(407) 655-8490
Flower arrangements

Natural Selections
Derwood, MD 20855
(301) 948-6453
By appointment only
Dried flower arrangements

Nature's Creations
302 Ridgefield Ct.
Asheville, NC 28806
1-800-450-0588
Fruit and vegetable candles

C.M. Offray Ribbons
(908) 879-4700
Ribbons

Paper Harvest
4723 Cherokee Trail
Dallas, TX 75209
(214) 351-1425
Paper doilies

Perin-Mowen
(212) 219-3937
Beeswax candles

Simpson & Turner Ltd.
1-800-239-3111
Freeze-dried flowers

Mrs. John L. Strong
Barney's
660 Madison Ave.
New York, NY 10021
(212) 826-8900
Fine engraved stationery

Talas
568 Broadway
New York, NY 10012
(212) 219-0770
Acid-free tissue paper

Viking Woodcrafts, Inc.
1317 8th St., S.E.
Waseca, MN 56093
1-800-328-0116
Candleshades and carriers

The Well-Furnished Garden
(301) 469-6879
By appointment only
Antique tableware

Flower Shows

Visiting flower shows always results in new ideas for arranging flowers and designing the garden.

UNITED STATES

Akron-Canton Home &
  Flower Show
John S. Knight Center
Akron, OH 44308
(216) 865-6700

Ann Arbor Flower &
  Garden Show
Washtenaw Farm Council
  Grounds
5055 Ann Arbor–Saline Rd.
Ann Arbor, MI 48104
(313) 998-7002

Cincinnati Flower &
  Garden Show
Ault Park
5090 Observatory Circle
Cincinnati, OH 45208
(800) 670-6808

Maymont Flower &
  Garden Show
Richmond Center
Fifth St. & Marshall
Richmond, VA 23220
(804) 358-7166

Minneapolis Home &
  Garden Show
Minneapolis Convention Center
1301 S. Second Ave.
Minneapolis, MN 55403
(612) 933-3850

Nashville Lawn & Garden Show
Tennessee State Fairgrounds
Nashville, TN 37242
(615) 352-3863

National Home & Garden Show
International Exhibition Center
Cleveland, OH 44135
(216) 529-1300

New England Spring
  Flower Show
Bayside Exposition Center
Boston, MA 02125
(617) 536-9280

New Jersey Flower &
  Garden Show
Garden State Exhibit Center
Somerset, NJ 08873
(909) 919-7660

Newport Flower Show
Newport, RI 02840
(401) 847-1000 #40

New York Flower Show
New York Coliseum
New York, NY 10020
(914) 421-3293

Northwest Flower &
  Garden Show
Washington State Convention
  & Trade Center
Ninth St. & Pike
Seattle, WA 98101
(206) 789-5333

Philadelphia Flower Show
Philadelphia Civic Center
34th St. & Civic Center Blvd.
Philadelphia, PA 19104
(215) 625-8253

Rhode Island Spring
  Flower Show
Rhode Island Convention Center
1 Sabin St.
Providence, RI 02903
(401) 421-7811

Rockefeller Center Garden &
  Flower Show
W. 48th to 51st St.
New York, NY 10020
(212) 632-3975

San Francisco Landscape &
  Garden Show
Herbst & Festival Pavilions
Fort Mason Center
San Francisco, CA 94123
(415) 750-5108

Southeastern Flower Show
Town Hall Exhibition Center
Atlanta, GA 30309
(404) 888-5638

St. Louis Flower Show
Cervantes Convention Center
801 Convention Plaza
St. Louis, MO 63101
(314) 569-3117

Washington Flower Garden
Washington Convention Center
900 9th St., N.W.
Washington, DC 20001
(703) 569-7174

ENGLAND

Hampton Court Palace
  Flower Show
East Molesey
Surrey, England
171-344-4444

Chelsea Flower Show
Royal Horticultural Society
London, England
171-834-4333
1-800-669-8687

ITALY

Tre Giorni per Il Giardino
Masino, Italy
11-66-04-339

FRANCE

L' Art du Jardin
Parc de Saint-Cloud
Paris, France
1-470-43-912

Journées des Plantes
Courson, France
331-64-58-9012

Historic Houses and Gardens

Inspiration and ideas for both house and garden abound at the places on this list, which you will enjoy visiting.

UNITED STATES

Alabama

Birmingham Botanic Garden
2612 Lane Park Dr.
Birmingham, AL 35223
(205) 879-1227

California

Filoli
Canada Rd.
Woodside, CA 94062
(415) 364-2880

J. Paul Getty Museum
17985 Pacific Coast Hwy.
Malibu, CA 90265
(213) 458-2003

The Huntington
   Botanical Gardens
1151 Oxford Rd.
San Marino, CA 91108
(818) 405-2124

La Mirada
720 Via Mirada
Monterey, CA 93940
(408) 372-3689

Virginia Robinson Gardens
1008 Elden Way
Beverly Hills, CA 90210
(310) 276-5367

Connecticut

Gertrude Jekyll Garden
Glebe House Museum
Hollow Rd.
Woodbury, CT 06798
(203) 263-2855

Delaware

Nemours Mansion & Gardens
Rockland Road
Wilmington, DE 19899
(302) 651-6912

Winterthur Museum
   Garden & Library
Route 52
Winterthur, DE 19735
1-800-448-3883

District of Columbia

Dunbarton Oaks
1703 32nd St., N.W.
Washington, DC 20007
(202) 342-3200

Hillwood Museum
4155 Linnean Ave., N.W.
Washington, DC 20008
(202) 686-8500

Georgia

Callaway Gardens
P.O. Box 2000
Pine Mountain, GA 31822
1-800-Callaway

Louisiana

Longue Vue House & Gardens
7 Bamboo Rd.
New Orleans, LA
(504) 488-5488

Maryland

Homewood House Museum
The Johns Hopkins University
3400 N. Charles St.
Baltimore, MD 21218
(410) 516-5589

Ladew Topiary Gardens
3535 Jarrettsville Pike
Monkton, MD 21111
(410) 557-9570

William Paca House
186 Prince George St.
Annapolis, MD 21401
(410) 263-5553

Massachusetts

Chesterwood
Off Route 183
Stockbridge, MA 01262
(413) 298-3579

Historic Deerfield
Off Routes 5 & 10
Deerfield, MA 01342
(413) 774-5581

Hancock Shaker Village
Routes 20 & 41
Pittsfield, MA 01201
(413) 443-0188

New Jersey

Duke Gardens Foundation
Somerville, NJ 08876
(201) 722-3700

New York

Boscobel Restoration
Route 9D
Garrison, NY 10524
(914) 265-3638

The Cloisters
Fort Tryon Park
New York, NY 10040
(212) 923-3700

Mills Mansion
Old Post Rd.
Staatsburg, NY 12580
(914) 889-4100

Montgomery Place
River Road
Annandale on Hudson,
   NY 12504
(914) 758-5461

New York Botanical Garden
200th St. at Southern Blvd.
Bronx, NY 10458
(718) 817-8700

Old Westbury Gardens
710 Old Westbury Rd.
Old Westbury, NY 11568
(516) 333-0048

Vanderbilt Mansion
Italian Gardens
Route 9
Hyde Park, NY 12538
(914) 229-7770

Wave Hill
Independence Ave. at 249th St.
Bronx, NY 10471
(718) 549-3200

North Carolina

Biltmore
1 North Park Sq.
Asheville, NC 28801
1-800-543-2961

Oregon

Washington Park International
Rose Test Garden
Washington Park
Portland, OR 97201
(503) 823-3636

Pennsylvania

Longwood Gardens
U.S. 1, P.O. Box 501
Kennett Square, PA 19348
(610) 388-6741

South Carolina

Drayton Hall
Highway 61
Charleston, SC 29414
(803) 766-0188

Magnolia Plantation & Gardens
Highway 61
Charleston, SC 29407
(803) 571-1266

Middleton Place
Highway 61
Charleston, SC 29407
(803) 556-6020
1-800-782-3608

Texas

Dallas Arboretum &
Botanical Garden
8525 Garland Rd.
Dallas, TX 75218
(214) 327-8263

National Wildflower
Research Center
4801 La Crosse
Austin, TX 78739
(512) 292-4200

Vermont

Historic Hildene
Route 7A
Manchester Village, VT 05254
(802) 362-1788

Virginia

Agecroft Hall
4305 Sulgrave Rd.
Richmond, VA 23221
(804) 848-4241
1-800-353-4241

Gunston Hall
Lorton, VA 22079
(703) 550-9220

Monticello
Route 53
Charlottesville, VA 22902
(804) 984-9822

Mt. Vernon
Mt. Vernon, VA 22121
(703) 780-2000

Oatlands
Route 2, Box 352
Leesburg, VA 22075
(703) 777-3174

Shirley Plantation
Charles City, VA 23030
(804) 829-5121

Williamsburg
P.O. Box 1776
Williamsburg, VA 23187
(804) 229-1000
1-800-History

In my book Antiques at Home, *I listed several associations of historic homes and gardens that you could write to in order to obtain information on the stately country houses for which Britain and France are known. A visit to any one of them can be an inspiration, as they feature the best in antiques and treasures and the finest in garden design.*

ENGLAND

English Heritage
P.O. Box 43
South Ruislip
Middlesex, England

Georgian Group
6 Fitzroy Square
London, England W1P 6DX

Historic Houses Association
38 Ebury St.
London, England SW1W OLU

The National Garden Scheme
Charitable Trust
57 Lower Belgrave St.
London, England SW1

The National Trust
36 Queen Anne's Gate
London, England SW1

Treasure Houses of England
Bedford Estates
29A Montague St.
London, England WC1

FRANCE

Caisse Nationale et des Sites
Hôtel de Sully
62, rue Saint-Antoine
Paris, France 75004

La Demeure Historique
55, quai de la Tournelle
Paris, France 75005